To Manage or Not, That Is the Question

Wiemer Renkema

# TO MANAGE OR **NOT,** THAT IS THE **QUESTION**

Dilemmas at work?
Ask *Shakespeare*

Translated
by
Patricia Daniels
& Cintia Taylor

# CONTENT

- **Brutus**: Roman senator who is very easily persuaded to stab a knife in the chest of his friend Julius Caesar.

- **Cassio**: sweet boy, good in math, in the service of the Venetian army under the command of Othello.

- **CEO**: leader of a random multinational somewhere in the world who has to do the right thing.

- **Cordelia**: too honest youngest daughter of the old King Lear.

- **Desdemona**: Othello's way too young sweetheart.

- **Director**: director of a random company in a random place in a random country.

- **Emilia**: feminist maid of Othello with her heart on her sleeve.

- **Fool**: authentic and stubborn extrovert who likes to hold a mirror in front of your face.

- **Hamlet**: prince of Denmark and indecisive son of a dead king.

- **HR-advisor**: helps the HR-manager in a random company in a random place.

- **HR-manager**: responsible for human resources in a random company in a random place.

- **Iago**: manipulator and Plotter in the service of the Venetian army under the command of Othello.

- **Julius Caesar**: Roman dictator suffering from

megalomania stabbed with a knife in his chest.

- **Kent**: management consultant of King Lear.

- **King Henry V**: former alcoholic and whoremonger who nevertheless developed himself to be a tremendous leader.

- **King Lear**: deluded old man who is too attached to his throne.

- **Lady Macbeth**: ambitious, power-thirsty woman who stops at nothing to get what she wants.

- **Macbeth**: a leader with power but without morality.

- **Manager**: (usually) solves problems and (usually) transforms opportunities into results.

- **Management consultant**: (generally

speaking) independent thinker who gives leaders a little push in the back.

- **One colleague**: your colleague (with a random profession) who's never short of a story.

- **Othello**: African general in the Venetian army with little empathy.

- **The other colleague**: your other colleague (with a random profession) who is really good at listening.

- **VP or vice president**: a random member of a random board of directors of a multinational somewhere in the world.

# PROLOGUE

*"All the world's a stage, and all the men and women merely players. They have their exits and their entrances and one man in his time plays many parts."*

**As you like it**

Each organisation is a theatre and every employee is an actor. Think of the dramas after the review process or when the promotions have been awarded. The fight for power in the executive room. The gossip at the coffee machine. The 'secret' romances after the Friday afternoon drink. Colleagues giggling about a manager's vanity. Disgruntled and worried workers in the corridor if the results are not as expected. It is all drama and comedy and has a lot of similarities with Shakespeare's plays. Even though they are over four hundred years old, his ideas about leadership, male / female relationships, deceit and communication are reflected in modern organisations. Fortunately, some things have changed in those four centuries. Failing leadership does not cost you by definition your head, but only your job. Being tarred and feathered has been replaced by anonymous nitwits on social media, and banishment in today's words is called being laid off. We should be glad that the physical workplace of today shows little similarities to how it used to be: working seven days a week from sunrise to sunset; no collective bargaining agreements, contracts or insurance; deplorable working conditions with a small wage as a reward. Okay, sure, employees can drink beer all day but only because you cannot drink the water. Whether the stage is a construction pit, an office or a restaurant, there are valuable lessons to be learned from the theatre in general and its characters in particular.

As an actor, I once played an Amsterdam working class version of Cassio in Shakespeare's *Othello*. This play is about envy and treason and gave me to the idea for this book. Aren't we all working in a Shakespeare play? Secretary, carpenter or waiter: aren't we all actors and isn't our office, our construction pit, and our restaurant a big theatre? Based on my experiences as both a HR Manager in several large organisations and on stage as a fanatic amateur theatre player, I started to investigate what we could learn from Shakespeare's plays.

Imagination, adaptability, creativity and effective communication are all important in every organisation to get good results. Organisations can learn from the theatre: from the actors and the director or from the plot and the lines. Albert Einstein understood this very well. He claimed that imagination is more important than knowledge since knowledge is about everything that is already here, while imagination points to everything that is going to come. The works of Shakespeare are not about the past, but about the here and now and everything that is about to happen. The characters in his plays now have a job in modern organisations. The emotions they exhibit have not changed in the past four centuries and are still easy to recognise: ambition, deception, love, envy, distrust and desire. He was a linguistic artist who added hundreds of words to the English language in the course of his career. Some words such as manager, employment and negotiate are still used in organisations. William Shakespeare is far ahead of his time. He is innovative, unconventional, and, consequently, unprecedentedly successful.

Employees and management can learn about their organisation while reviewing Shakespeare as there are so many similarities. Mighty families are powerful organisations. The king is the CEO. Counts and chancellors are the management and the 17th century serf is the employee of today. That is called progress. Shakespeare lives in a time of many changes. The catholic Church has just been replaced by the Anglican Church, which made quite an impressive case of organisational change. Two families fighting for the throne are the same as two rival organisations wanting to take over the same company. An arranged marriage can easily be seen as a hostile take-over. Shakespeare's political and social observations are quite common and therefore still applicable. History and fantasy are the safest choices for Shakespeare, avoiding to express himself about morals, politics and religion. In those days, it was better for your neck.

Like any Shakespearean play, this book has five acts. By using Shakespeare, you will discover what you can learn about Henry V's leadership, what Lady Macbeth has to say about diversity, how Cordelia tries to keep her integrity, what King Lear can tell you about communication and how Othello makes a mess of a promotion - topics every organisation struggles with and topics that you, the employee, are confronted with day in and day out. I combine the insights of Shakespeare with those of modern day (management) theories. The similarities are amazing!

Whether or not you know anything about Shakespeare or have read some of his plays, you will enjoy reading this book. It's about you and about me, about the organisations in which we work and how we all have a little Hamlet, Othello or Macbeth hidden inside. And yes, that is a label and occasionally I am using that. Not just a box for you, but also for your colleagues and your managers. I use them for clarification, to make something larger than life or at least larger than your daily working environment. I understand this can be annoying at times but rest assured that the door of your box remains open and there is no lock. Each act also contains a number of dialogues from own past experience. You can come up with a name for the CEO, the other colleague and the HR advisor who are playing a role in these dialogues – if a name does not already pop up immediately. That being said, any resemblance to existing persons and organisations is merely coincidental.

I believe in imagination and, like Shakespeare in his plays, I do not explain everything. Now that you have this book in your hands it is your book and it is up to you to read and learn whatever you like. What role will you give yourself?

*"All the world's a stage, and all the men and women merely players. They have their exits and their entrances and one man in his time plays many parts."*

ACT 1

**DIRECTIO**

OR **ENSEMBLE?**

*"The labour we delight in physics pain."*

***Macbeth***

In a play, an actor has a role. In an organisation, an employee has a role. Shakespeare writes his plays having one major advantage: all characters arise from his imagination. On the basis of structure and plot of the play he created characters and if a turn was needed, he would come up with just one more. That is the advantage of poetic freedom. This is not possible in modern organisations as these teams often grow organically. People come in, others leave. People grow, evolve and have highs and lows in their performance. If certain competencies are not present, an additional character can be created, for example a temp or interim manager. Managers have the opportunity to recruit someone complementary to the team only when someone leaves or if the organisation is growing.

The strongest links on stage are the director, the cast and the collaboration among the actors. The first part of this act is about the directors of an organisation: their leaders and managers. What is each of their unique roles and what is the difference between them? The second part is about collaboration and the difference between good and bad teams. To illustrate this, I use the play Henry V which deals with leadership and teams, in this case an army. Finally, you will read about the division of roles, the characters. There are six distinct archetypes in the plays of Shakespeare. I challenge you to identify which character you are in your team. The different characters in a play operate with the same emotions as workers in modern organisations. On stage and in the workplace, you see and feel every day envy, betrayal, love, friendship and betrayal.

Excellent leadership with effective management, an outstanding team, and your awareness of your role help an organisation move forward. These are three of the strongest links in a team.

## THE DIRECTOR

"Uneasy lies the head that wears the crown," says Henry IV in Shakespeare's play by the same name. Many CEOs and directors will recognise that feeling of discomfort. The symbol of leadership in Shakespeare's time is the crown. Leadership is a major theme in his plays, which teach valuable lessons on this subject. Ironically, the most important lesson may well be: don't become a leader. The fate of most kings, princes, and generals in his plays is not very attractive. Betrayal, a deadly curse, or being poisoned are but a few of the ingredients in Shakespeare's work that will take away your lust for power or willingness to raise your hand for a leading role.

Shakespeare asks many questions about leadership. But two in particular catch the eye. The first one is: what makes a leader successful? And the second one is: what can make him or her stumble? These two questions determine the course and outcome of his plays. The answers to the questions are applicable to any modern organisation. They speak to the quality of the leadership and the results the organisation is able to achieve.

According to Shakespeare, successful leaders rely on their intuition. His most successful leaders dare to do just that and make the right decisions. A successful leader is decisive. He is, after all, paid to make decisions. A leader does not lend his ear to the sycophants around him. He knows that anyone who dares to say no will be of added value to achieve his goals. When it comes to what makes a leader trip, Shakespeare is very clear: ambition without morality. You will lose your head (in his plays, literally) if you make your way to the top at any cost. Another hurdle is gossip and slander. They are the worst counsellors. A good leader knows to ignore these as they will make you stumble.

Ironically, it is the hard fate that Shakespeare has in store for most of his leaders that teach us some of the most valuable leadership lessons. In Henry V Shakespeare writes about inspiring yet ruthless leadership.

*In his younger years Henry roams the streets of London. He has bad friends, drinks too much, has sex with the* wrong kind of women, and shows little if any interest in the monarchy. His father, Henry IV, almost gives up on him. Henry gets quite an education about the fringes of society. We would perhaps recognise him in the rebellious period of UK's Prince Harry, or in the college years of the current Dutch King, Willem Alexander. It is this very familiarity with the ways and values of the 'commoner' that enables Henry to become a powerful king idolised by his soldiers - much to his father's dismay. Once king, Henry sets his sights on recapturing France. He is confronted with devilish dilemmas and his integrity as a leader is severely challenged. With no less than five French soldiers on every Englishman, he is faced with an almost impossible task. However, Henry's cunning strategy enables him to motivate his troops to unprecedented performance thus winning decisively over the French. Henry V is a leader who speaks the language of his soldiers and that enables him to gain their trust. Just before the decisive battle he inspires his soldiers: "Once more unto the breach, my friends, once more!"

## AN EXCELLENT LEADER

Shakespeare introduces different leadership styles into his plays. In the 17th century the democratic and coaching styles of leadership are not yet hip and happening, but other styles are. The leadership of Henry V is an example of a relationship-oriented leadership style. He believes in collaboration, innovation and knows he must inspire to motivate. Sometimes the situation - in Henry's case, the approaching and decisive battle with the French - requires a different style of leadership to be successful. This comes to surface in Henry's last meeting with his generals, shortly before the battle. These generals, who are more or less his management team, know the enemy outnumbers them and urge Henry to expand the army with more soldiers. Henry, the commander-in-chief, is having none of it and lets his authority speak. He reveals his plan of attack and is able to convince his generals. He tells them exactly what to do (working together), how they will do it (with a new and innovative weapon) and what he will do to help them. He is focused on the relationship, but doesn't tolerate any contradiction. His operating motto "the fewer men, the greater share of honour," motivates and engages his generals to follow his direction. Henry V faces multiple risks. His soldiers - already tired to the bone and outnumbered by the enemy – might run away to avoid the battlefield, his generals may turn against him, and he can lose to the French army. Henry dares to take these risks because he is confident his plan will work and he trusts his army. Intuitively, he also feels that the enemy is underestimating them and that could be a game changer.

In many commercial organisations, you see a similar pressure: the operating result is to be achieved with minimal staff and resources. This way, the result (profit) by means of a dividend or a bonus will be shared with as few people as possible. CEOs, driven by profit maximisation, take a similar risk as Henry. Since this can backfire, not every leader will be victorious with such an attitude. Doing more with fewer people may result in exhausted and demotivated staff. It could cause top managers turning their backs on the organisation because they are disgruntled but mainly due to a lack of confidence in their leadership.

CEOs who demonstrate the same appetite for risk as

Henry does, do well in following his teachings. Henry takes responsibility for his decisions, monitors the execution of tasks closely, and listens to other people's ideas. Henry shows how, depending on the situation, a relationship-oriented leadership style and authoritative style complement and reinforce each other. The speech of Henry V motivates his officers and soldiers to make the impossible possible. Some CEOs are able to do the same. Strong leadership is a unique quality. Exceptional leadership, like that of Henry V is a rarity. Companies and organisations, regardless of size, need a leader.

## TO LEAD IS TO SUFFER

Leadership is not an easy task. It is demanding and comes with and leads to many uncertainties. Consequently, that is a major difference between a leader and a manager: a leader can deal with these uncertainties; while a manager not necessarily.

Too often the words leader and manager are used interchangeably, but they are different. In fact, the difference between a leader and a manager is not subtle. It is always visible and tangible in any organisation. It's present in any office, it's in the details of a fancy suit, or the stripes on a uniform. To whom do people listen? To whom do they ask their questions? Or, most importantly, who do they trust?

Managers are primarily concerned with material activities such as planning, budgeting and staff activities. Leaders take a strategic approach to guide their organisation into the future. A leader solves dilemmas and the manager deals with the resulting issues. Leadership is about vision, change and behaviour. Leaders are not necessarily at the top of the pyramid and the managers underneath. Leadership is not specific to an organisational level. The difference is mainly in what the leader does: the right thing. A leader sees the future and creates opportunities, management transforms these opportunities into results.

## SCENE 1

(A conference room in a random office in a random city. The director sits at a table surrounded by the management team. The mood is tense.)

**The director**: Our company is in dire straits. We

are up to our necks in problems and I cannot wait any longer to intervene. If I do nothing, the future is highly uncertain.

(After a long silence)

**A manager**: What do you suggest?

The director: I do not want anyone in this company, and I mean really nobody, including you and me, to get a salary increase this year. Only this way we can ensure that our profit goes back to an acceptable level and we make our shareholders happy.

**A manager**: Aren't you afraid that this will kill motivation? That our colleagues are dissatisfied and might go work somewhere else? Most have worked hard this year.

**The director**: That's a risk I'm willing to take. If they want to leave, then they should simply go. Fine with me and works miracles on the cost side …

(Another long silence)

**A manager**: And how will you tell them?

The director: I'm not going to tell them anything at all. I have you guys to do just that.

(Everyone stares at the table in front of him, the

silence is killing)

**A manager**: Um, but, uh, don't you think it would be better that the message comes from you. All colleagues hear the same voice? Yours?

**The director**: No, I do not think so.

**A manager**: You might still agree that it is something worthwhile to consider. To me it seems that ...

(The director interrupts him, furious now)

**The director**: We are a team, damn it, and if you do not do what I say you can get the hell out of here.

The director in this scene does not tolerate contradiction. He does not ask questions, speaks mainly for himself and tries to avoid taking his responsibility. It is a compelling leadership style that is not exceptional but with limited effectiveness. It is typical for managers who 'accidentally' end up in a leadership role. The director is trying to manage a dilemma while solving a problem. It is as if he has an identity crisis and does not know whether to manage or to lead - whether or not he is capable of the latter remains to be seen. He seems to have little or no confidence in his management team, not even if a manager shows leadership and dares to ask a question. This compelling style is reminiscent of the kings in Shakespeare's plays who believe they have a divine right to rule. A director, with this style, consciously or not, risks discouraging his employees. Management as a healthy counterweight to leadership is lacking in this organisation. There is little support for his decision from the colleagues who have to carry it out: the management. The director has no vision, explains nothing, does not help his colleagues and is therefore not able to convince nor inspire.

## SCENE 2

(An office in any office in any city. The director enters.)

**The director**: That was not so pretty yesterday.

**The manager**: No, that's quite an understatement Adrian.

**The director**: It derailed.

**The manager**: Yes.

(A long silence)

**The manager**: What's next?

(The director strolls and stares into space)

**The manager**: Damn it, Adrian. Should I go out and find another job? Frankly, I'm not sure what I'm doing here.

**The director**: Hmm … mmm ...

**The manager**: You just cannot sell it this way to the organisation.

**The director**: You might need some time to think that over. You know where to find me.

This constitutes a breach of trust between the director and the manager. In contrast to the first scene, the director does not invoke his organisational role as decision maker but at the same time he does not know how to handle the situation. There is a palpable fear; the director does not have the skills (and perhaps not even the knowledge) to deal with this conflict. The manager still extends his hand, shows initiative and takes responsibility but received a negative response. The two are not aligned making it highly uncertain whether they will be able to hold together the organisation. Something is broken and the half-hearted attempt by the director to fix this is not working. The director lacks some essential skills to adapt his leadership style to the situation. Consequently, he is not acting with confidence in his role. It is a misunderstanding to think that every manager needs to be a leader. Or that every manager can learn to become a leader for that matter. Most teams can function quite well with only a manager or someone who is accountable for the results of the team. Some managers are leaders, most just manage and that is fine. An organisation does not need that many leaders anyway.

## HENRY TEACHES YOU A LESSON

In his young and brash years Henry learned that you need a team of motivated people around you to be successful - motivated individuals who can give you feedback, from whom you can learn to continue to develop yourself. Based on experience he knows that you have to give them confidence, so that in turn they trust you. A leader has a clear vision and strategy for colleagues to follow. Henry wants to recapture France and has a plan to be successful, even with far fewer soldiers. Nevertheless, he knows how to motivate his troops to stand behind him on the battlefield. An excellent leader is open to unconventional solutions; he is innovative. Henry uses pointed stakes to lure the French cavalry into an ambush. Are you not innovative yourself? Make sure you have creative people on your team. To gauge the mood of his troops, the king mingles in disguise with his soldiers to talk to them. He is interested and concerned about their success and well-being. A good leader observes things directly and trusts the information he can gather himself.

A good leader is not afraid to say farewell to an employee who does not share his values or has a different goal in mind. If coaching does not work anymore and there are no other career opportunities, you have no other choice. Henry sends an old friend to early retirement (read: bans him) and another one, who was his drinking pal in earlier days, was fired (read: executed). Henry knows he must encourage his troops to make the impossible possible and tells them, "Old men forget, yet all shall be forgot, but he'll remember, with advantages, what feats he did that day (...) be in their flowing cups remembered (...) from this day to the ending of the world but we in it shall be remembered. We few, we happy few, we band of brothers for he today that sheds his blood with me, shall be my brother; but he ne'er so vile, this day shall gentle his condition. And gentlemen in England now abed, shall think themselves accursed they were not here and hold their manhoods cheap whiles any speaks this fought with us upon Saint Crispin's day." That is quite a difference compared to a simple 'come on boys, let's get to work.' A manager does not need to be as articulate as Henry. In particular, it is up to the leaders of an organisation to inspire and motivate the employees as a group, and above all to create confidence. Who wears the crown with pleasure? That is the secret to the happiness of the employees and consequently yours.

## COLLABORATION

Working in teams, especially a high performing team, has many advantages. An excellent team innovates faster, learns from the mistakes they make, and finds better solutions to problems. Generally, people work better in teams and have more job satisfaction when they work together. Human beings are social by nature. Successful organisations are concerned not only with how people work but how they work together. What makes a team successful? How do you achieve results together? That's what we will delve into in detail now.

## THE DRAMA OF THE EXCELLENT TEAM

An excellent team is built on mutual trust and conflict resolution. In excellent teams people know their role and take responsibility for individual and collective results. It is built like a pyramid where trust is the foundation. Without trust, there won't be any great results. Lack of trust among colleagues will result in an unsafe environment: the fear of being punished for what you say. A good and open discussion where everyone can speak up will not be possible. Without trust, there will be a lack of commitment and no one will dare to take responsibility – everyone will be afraid to fail. Trust is about openness, the ability to communicate honestly, and being allowed to make mistakes without being punished.

Henry and his army are successful because there is confidence in the leadership and strategy.

*Figure 1. Characteristics of a strong team (Lencioni)*

The most important thing Henry does is show his vulnerability. With his daring attack, he puts his throne and his reputation at stake. He is not afraid of losing face, thus giving the rest of the army the opportunity to do the same. Henry doesn't hesitate to confront his generals if they disagree on the number of soldiers needed. Consequently, the generals are not fearful of asking for more soldiers. That too is a matter of trusting one another. Once the decision is made to attack the French each and every one of them takes responsibility and executes their tasks

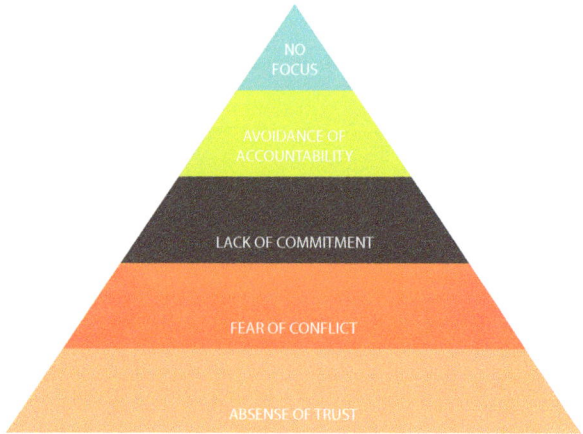

*Figure 2. Characteristics of a weak team (Lencioni)*

beyond what could be expected. Everyone has only one objective: chop the French army into pieces. This is the only way the ultimate result – in this case a glorious victory – can be achieved.

Without trust a team will not be successful. A team with lack of confidence is too frightened to get into an argument, which leads to the inability of solving any conflicting issues. Managers and employees run away from their responsibilities, resulting in little to no attention to the results that need to be achieved.

The managers in scenes 1 and 2 have no confidence in their director and they are probably not the only ones in the management team. It is not a safe place to speak up. If you do, the director will retaliate verbally. His abusive behaviour signals that he is afraid of having a discussion with his managers. He does ask them to commit to his decision and be the ones who sell it to the employees. The big question is what his team is going to do with that responsibility. They are likely to avoid it. Because there is no confidence and no room for discussion, there is no basis to support the director's decision to scrap salary increases. The results of this all? Managers who bring different messages to their teams or make exceptions to the rule 'as we really cannot afford this excellent manager to go to the competition.' Organisations end up with sulking teams, without focus on what they should be doing, and a demotivated management team.

## AN EXCELLENT TEAM

An excellent team consists of employees who are conscious of their role in that team. In a team, you play three roles: a professional one, an organisational one and a personal role. Henry is commander-in-chief of his army and has a certain level of expertise with which he can lead his men into battle. This is his professional role resulting from his organisational role as king of England. His personal role is the distinctive way he behaves – he is close to the infantry. He associates with them as he learned in the slums of London at a young age. In turn, this knowledge, gained from his personal role, contributes to his professional role, completing the circle.

It is important that your individual qualities match the role you have as closely as possible. The team's success partly depends on that. This is applicable not only to directors and managers but to everyone in an organisation. The trapeze artist in the circus does not work with the lions, neither can you ask the French teacher to replace their Geography colleague. Based on your personality, knowledge, and skills you will have some favourite roles that fit you well. Your awareness of these preferences is essential for you to function effectively. For example, as an individual, you may be focused more on others than on yourself; you may be a thinker or a doer; you may want to give direction or you may prefer to be given direction. In an excellent team, there is a balance between the various roles. You should complement not compete with your colleagues. The challenge is to put a team together in such a way that an optimal result can be achieved. If you only have thinkers on a team it is likely that there are so many ideas that implementation is delayed or does not happen at all. If there are only doers in a team they may compete for the available work with a misguided result. You need practical people, but also colleagues who are able to make connections in a group. The unique qualities of each individual and how they complement each other make the difference between a good and an excellent team.

## A STANDING OVATION

Although actors are known for their individuality, their interplay on stage with other actors is of crucial importance. Without teamwork, the audience is not captivated by the performance and the actors receive no applause. The ensemble is a real team. Mutual trust is important starting with the rehearsal process - for example, you are counting on your fellow actors to know their lines. Conflicts may arise about the acting, the staging, or the interpretation of the texts. So the actors will need to come together under the leadership of the director to resolve any issues. Without mutual trust, there will be no solutions to these challenges, resulting in an armed peace on stage. This will put pressure on the dedication to the play: the actors will not provide the spotlight to each other anymore. Dedication is what fuels the energy necessary for each actor to give their everything every night. Sharing this energy with each other is a huge responsibility during the performance. A mentally absent actor or actress on stage may result in a dramatic evening - but not the kind of drama the public wants to see. A play is one of the most extreme forms of teamwork. That is why actors come together at the end of a play to jointly receive the applause of the audience. Excellent teams have a common purpose, a higher value for which they want to work and - in Shakespeare's time - fight for together. More importantly, they also know why and for whom they do it.

## THE CAST

Shakespeare created a substantial number of characters over the years for his plays. Many of these
characters can be categorised into six archetypes
that have a specific role in his plays. The layout of
the six archetypes in the quadrant below is based on
the loyalty that they show to, for example, the king.
You will see these archetypes throughout your organisation and in your team. They provide insight into
the role of the employee in the organisation. This
could be you or perhaps you recognise a colleague. To
what extent does someone pursue his own interests,
perhaps at the expense of the team and the organisation? How effective is this role within the team?
In other words: what is the balance between what is
in it for the employee and what they will bring to a
team, to an organisation? The characters of Shakespeare are 'larger than life'. As are these archetypes.
They are over exaggerated, just to make them bigger and thus more recognizable. Which character are
you?

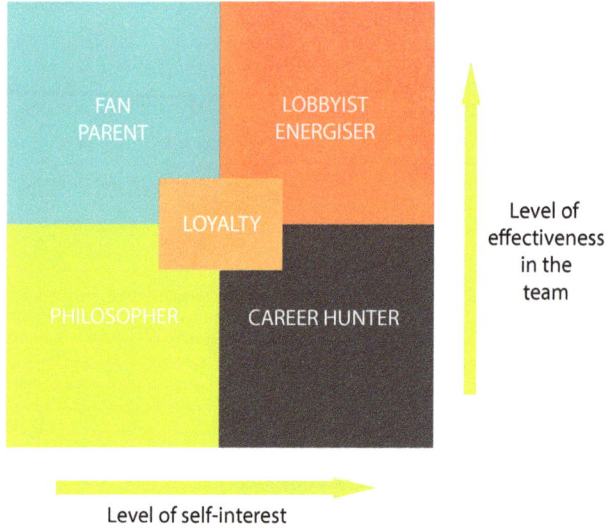

*Figure 3. The six organisational roles (Veith)*

## THE FAN CHEERS FOR EVERYONE

The Fans are very dedicated workers and they identify themselves completely with the organisation. They don't ask questions and simply execute what is asked of them. They are hard workers for whom their work is basically their life. Fans strive for unity and, as a result, prevent unnecessary tension and conflict in a team. They are the linking pin in a team. They don't like conflict and often have difficulty making decisions.

Every organisation has fans, which is good since every organisation needs them. The fans are the fundament of an organisation. There is often too little attention to this group of hard but sometimes anonymous workers because many organisations focus on their top talent only. They are selling this group short.

In one of Shakespeare's Roman tragedies we see a typical example of a fan. A loyal servant would do anything for his emperor and loses as many as 20 of his sons on the battlefield (yes, that is a lot but it is fiction and drama). He brings gold and jewellery to the emperor and believes that hard and dedicated work will pay off. He forgets that networking and politics are equally important to move up the organisation's ladder. The Fan is a tad naive. In the end, the servant is killed simply because he has no sons left and there is nothing else he can do for the emperor. A major risk is the Fan turning against the organisation when the reality sets in that there will not be a reward. Fans may take unwarranted risks to get the appreciation they feel they deserve. Many whistle-blowers are former fans. If you are a Fan, you need to stand up for yourself. Do not wait until you get praised. Don't expect the reward to come your way automatically. You may have to wait a very, very long time. For a manager, it is therefore important not to take the Fans for granted but to ensure they get rewarded, appreciated, and that you lend them an ear. If you are lucky there are a few Fans around you at work. Compliment them on their loyalty and their work. They will like that.

## THE PARENT WILL TAKE CARE OF YOU

The Parent is the one wearing the 'seen it, done it' t-shirt and has the attitude to go with it. The Parent knows the organisation inside out and has a large network. These colleagues often play an important role in supporting the management and search continuously for mutual interests in the group in order to get everyone going in the same direction. Over the years, Parents earn the respect of their colleagues and assume this credit is infinite. They believe the organisation cannot do without them. Parents are so attached to the organisation that they become blind to the changes that are happening around them. Parents value the privileges accrued over the many years of service but have lost the ability to look objectively at their own performance. Taking a step back, even if it would be good for work-life balance would never come up in their mind. Consequently, Parents will never think about their succession. This is a major pitfall: they do not see changes to their position coming until it hits them in the face. Managers who have a Parent in their team will struggle to implement changes. In the eyes of a Parent you are rather quickly considered to be a traitor.

The famous Roman emperor Julius Caesar imagines himself untouchable and does not recognise that the people are turning against him. Change without his consent is simply unimaginable. On the day that would become his last on Earth, he dismisses the objections of his wife: "Danger knows that Caesar is more dangerous than he is." Brutus' knife thought differently.

## THE PHILOSOPHER IS PUZZLED

Philosophers are essential for any organisation but they come with a very elaborate user guide. Philosophers always need more information, love details and are consequently micromanaging anything they have to do. But taking decisions? No, they leave that to others – that is, if they are capable of handing over control. The Philosopher is an expert, fond of numbers and is open to the opinions of others, provided it is well-founded. They constantly worry about things that can go wrong and have a strong desire for perfection. They care for the people around them, although they will not always express it.

The Philosopher may be the 'dead weight' in a team, the person who is not necessarily opposing change but certainly not accelerating it. The Philosopher typically sees many obstacles on the road ahead and thinks of problems rather than solutions. Unfortunately, their behaviour may become contagious. Philosophers know so well what they are talking about that they are able to install doubt in the rest of the team.

Another problem arises when Philosophers question their future in the organisation. Demotivated and unproductive, they may stay longer than wished for, since leaving is too big of a deal to them. This is also contagious and a risk for the performance of the entire team. Hamlet, perhaps Shakespeare's most famous character, is a prime example of a Philosopher. "To be or not to be. That is the question." He can spend hours musing this question. Meanwhile his uncle kills his father, his mother remarries this uncle and he conducts conversations with the ghost of his father. He does not know what to do and an early and tragic death is the result of Hamlet's indecisiveness. 'Do not doubt' is an important Shakespeare lesson in leadership.

## THE CAREER HUNTER WANTS A TROPHY

Career Hunters are particularly concerned with their own careers. They are passionate and strong-willed, and have a strong urge to perform. These Hunters give direction and can initiate change. Career Hunters are not interested in the consequences of their actions for the team and the organisation. As long as the goals of the organisation fit with their ambitions they will contribute full of energy. Shakespeare wrote a lot about these people. Eager for power they hunt for the throne or another desirable position. They do not care for any casualties along the way. Everything must yield to the higher purpose and success knows no morality. The people around Career Hunters will eventually notice this and, over the years, they will increasingly make more enemies. It is not surprising that Career Hunter change their workplace every other year or so. They have no long-term strategy and work from success to success. Their definition of success may very well deviate from that of the organisation or colleagues. They could not care less. The Career Hunter always wants to outperform the competition and take the spotlight. No wonder this category has eminently superlatives like Silvio Berlusconi and Donald Trump. For these business men trophies were not enough and that is why they went hunting for political ones. In their view, even a woman is a trophy. This narcissistic hunter does not care for what hangs on the wall next to their favourite mirror. Because yes, most Career Hunters, especially in the superlative, are men.

# A LOBBYIST MAKES YOU THINK

'I do not want to meddle with anything but ...' are the favourite words of the Lobbyist. Shakespeare made much use of this role. Especially in his political dramas they were required to give a certain twist to the storyline.

Lobbyists busy themselves and are dedicated to influencing others. An organisation cannot do without a Lobbyist in its midst. As long as your Lobbyist is on your side, you have nothing to worry about. The Lobbyist feels the sentiment of employees and other stakeholders in great detail and is able to silence other parties with subtle arguments. The Lobbyist explains complex matters in simple words. There are times when the manipulator in the Lobbyist surfaces and tries to makes something right that is wrong. It is important for organisations to guard against such proclamations that could be a distraction from the things that are actually important. In organisations, you will find Lobbyists in the works council or near the coffee machine. They generate new ideas and alternatives to complex problems, but can be eccentric, radical or impractical.

## THE ENERGISER GOES CRAZY

The Energiser does not think but acts. Like the Career Hunter, Energisers will not stop until they have achieved their goal. Instinctively the Energiser does what is best; there is no room for doubt. Reflecting on their own actions is not even a consideration. The Energiser can be impatient and short tempered and provoke people with their behaviour. If rapid action needs to be taken, then you need Energisers on your team. The core attitude is simple: Let's do it! Fast! Now! The Energiser does not like to be entertained in long discussions with many numbers. If the Energiser is right a number of times, people are going to believe in their visionary powers. The ugly part of Energiser is that they have little understanding for others, are easily offended, and struggle to change direction. Famous Energisers in business are men like Elon Musk and Richard Branson. They draw their plan and build their companies with passion and in an innovative way. Steve Jobs was another famous Energiser. He had to say goodbye to his beloved Apple but got a second chance because Apple did not have an Energiser of his scale in the organisation. They simply could not do without Jobs because there was no credible alternative available.

## SO, I AM IN A BOX NOW?

No. The archetypes can be found in different places in their part of the quadrant. Not every Fan is necessarily very effective in the team and the Fans can sometimes sink to questionable performance. A Career Hunter can put their self-interest aside to do something good for the team and the Lobbyist is not always occupied with themselves. The big difference with the theatre is that at work you do not constantly have to worry about your role. The basis of the characters, the archetypes, the interests they pursue and the role in the team remains unchanged however. You, your colleagues and the roles you play may change just as in a Shakespeare play: a Fan slowly growing into the role of a Parent, a Philosopher who has had proper training turning into an Energiser or a Career Hunter who needs to slow down after a burnout. It's just as Shakespeare changes the personality of a character, depending on the direction the play needs to take. Henry V changed slowly after his battles in France from an Energiser into a Parent. And not only because he marries and becomes the father to the next Henry.

## THE KEY TO SUCCESS

Celebrating success together is one of the most important things you can do as an organisation. At one of my former employers, at the end of each month new customers were celebrated. Everyone who was involved, from sales to R&D, was present and received the recognition they deserved as a team. The popping of the champagne's bottle became a symbolic gesture, where the goal was to try to drive the cork into the ceiling as deep as possible. All the team members involved wrote their name around the hole that was created by the cork. This was visible to everyone each Friday afternoon when the week was closed off with drinks. After two years, the success of the organisation was not written on the wall but on the ceiling.

Many CEOs and executives find it difficult to hear that most people are more loyal to the team than to the company. Actually, they should be proud of this since it means that people in a team trust each other and dare to lean on each other. Good cooperation within the team leads to commitment. "The labour we delight in physics pain," says Macbeth. A team and each individual in that team will feel responsible for the final result. That makes them a strong link.

Leaders and managers bear a heavy responsibility. What brings out the best in the people you work with every day? If you are able to bring out the best, then you will quite rightfully wear that proverbial crown on your head. The beauty is that the crown suddenly feels a lot lighter too.

Shakespeare tells us that it is impossible to fight change. Whoever will nevertheless try to do so, will stumble and will become the weakest link. This is in stark contrast to Shakespeare's most successful leaders and managers who embrace change and support ideas that help progress. That makes them a strong link. For example, take Henry's words once more: "If we are marked to die, we are enough to do our country loss; and if to live, the fewer men, the greater share of honour. God's will, I pray thee wish not one man more. By Jove, I am not covetous for gold, it yearns me not if men my garments wear; such outward things dwell not in my desires. But if it be a sin to covet honour, I am the most offending soul alive."

And you? Who are you? An Energiser? A Philosopher? What is your contribution to the organisation where you work? Does your role fit you like a glove or does it pinch? If it pinches, ask yourself where and what you can do about it? Ask yourself: Who is rooting for me in the team? And do you cheer for someone else as well? What makes your role a strong link?

ACT 2

MAKE-U

OR **NATURAL?**

*"This above all: to thine own self be true, and it must follow, as the night the day, thou cannot be false to any man."*

**Hamlet**

Imagine: a play without different characters. Everyone on stage plays the same character and looks the same too. Wouldn't you be bored to death? Shakespeare created very diverse characters, each with their own particular role. The irony wants Shakespeare to be a white man and that in his plays only white men appear on stage; the stage was off limits for women. Four hundred years later, however, nobody is surprised to see a female Hamlet, a homosexual Lear, a disabled Julius Caesar or an elderly Romeo. For an organisation, that is no different: they also must embrace diversity. This means different people for different roles - creative and innovative - in order to be a good and successful employer.

Diversity is comprehensive. Religion, race, gender, personality, norms, values, culture, physical and mental health are a few concepts that are part of diversity in an organisation. It is about everything we see and all we do not see, such as personality and cognitive aspects as knowledge and skills. For example, gender, cultural background, and sexual preference say something about who you are but only to a limited extent. The real power of diversity is in what we do not see in someone's personality, know-ledge, and attitude. The different archetypes in Act 1 illustrate this. From the outside, it is not possible to see if anyone is a Career Hunter or a Philosopher, a Parent or a Lobbyist. From the outside, you can-not see what you can contribute to an organisation. Unless you are a model, bouncer, prostitute or a Hollywood icon.

Because Shakespeare wants his public to feel sympathy, compassion and love for his characters, equality, diversity and inclusion are important social values in his plays. The different characters complement each other and make the play vibrant and successful. Diversity in a play gives momentum and brings energy. It can change the plot and thus the direction. It is not so different in an organisation. Shakespeare's plays are an example of one of the main forces of diversity: changing direction and expanding options.

There are roughly three different forms of diversity that can be found in Shakespeare's plays.

The first form is the relationship between men and women with a leading role for Lady Macbeth. The second form is Mavericks. These are perhaps Shakespeare's favourite expressions of diversity. Shakespeare had a lot of fun with these crazy and extravagant characters, but most organisations find it very difficult to work with these outsiders. Henry V is a creative maverick who can be compared to innovative mavericks like Othello. Hamlet is an authentic maverick. The final scenes of this act deal with the last form of diversity: team diversity. Shakespeare used this form to portray powerful families. Some of them were very homogeneous and took one side against the common enemy. Other families who were very diverse caused mutual twists but could also be a source for success.

An organisation with diversity in its DNA feels like a warm bath for every employee who wants to be true to themselves and wants to develop their unique talents. Diversity creates new insights and a natural balance. A diverse organisation is more agile, changes direction more easily, and is therefore more creative and innovative than its competitors. Diversity provides energy, engagement, innovation. In a diverse organisation, employees feel at home and achieve results together. Diversity, in all its facets, is a permanent challenge for every organisation. But it pays off. Big time.

## F/M

For centuries, there was no room for women in organisations unless you happened to be queen. In the past hundred years that has changed rapidly and the workplace is no longer the exclusive domain of men. Women and men are easy to distinguish in the workplace, but they are not equally represented in every organisation. Nursery schools and the army are just a couple of examples of workplaces where the numbers are skewed. Prejudice plays a significant role when it comes to where men and women are positioned. Men are seen as diligent and fit to be soldiers. Women may be viewed as caring and consequently good with toddlers.

## SCENE 3

(A conference call between a HR manager in the New York head office and a HR advisor in London.)

**HR manager**: How was your trip to Milan? Did you have a good chat with Gianni?

**HR advisor**: Well, that's quite a story Liz. First, I had to wait for half an hour because, and now I am quoting his secretary, 'he has a very special guest for lunch'.

**HR manager**: Oh dear, is he still entertaining his mistresses in the office?

**HR advisor**: Certainly looks that way. A lady left his office looking rather messy in her appearance and he had a rather smug smile on his face.

(both laugh)

**HR manager**: That being said, have you been able

to discuss with him the importance of diversity in his team as we agreed?

**HR advisor**: Sure, but the conversation was rather peculiar, to say the least. It does not appear he has any feeling for the power of diversity. He did not even realise there is not a single woman in his team.

**HR manager**: That worries me.

**HR advisor**: I know. I am really not sure if I got to him.

**HR manager**: Why not?

**HR advisor**: Well, when I made a strong appeal for him to select a woman for the opening he has in his team his reaction was really, really odd.

**HR manager**: Odd? Tell me more, what did he say?

**HR advisor**: This will make you laugh Liz. He said (imitates a thick Italian accent): of course Paul, I understand. Every team needs a mama and the man cannot be the mama, so I will get a mama for my team.

**HR manager**: Oh boy.

Diversity and prejudice are often linked and let each other stumble, as in scene 3. Stereotypes and prejudices (e.g., women are caring) still play a role when it comes to the accessibility women have in organisations and the positions for which they are considered. Even in brand new office buildings, the glass ceiling is still part of the building plan.

## DIVERSITY IN SHAKESPEARE'S TIME

Elizabeth I was sitting on the throne when Shakespeare was writing his plays. She was a great admirer of his work, which was regularly showcased in her palace. Her father, Henry VIII, decided after his single son's death that a woman should be able to sit on the throne as well. That was something new for the English, and something they found really exciting. As Queen of England not only was she the head of state, she was also the commander of the army - another oddity for the English. The commoners had plenty of time to get used to female leadership: Elizabeth's reign lasted 45 years. In order to survive in a court full of intrigue, Elizabeth took on many so-called 'male' attributes or qualities throughout the course of her reign. For example, she used the word king when talking about herself, she cursed like a dock worker and occasionally threw a cup to someone's head when she was contradicted. Given that, it is not surprising that there was a theory that she was actually a man in women's clothes, perhaps a drag queen.

## LADY MACBETH: THE ROLE MODEL

Shakespeare's brilliant brain has given us some powerful women who play an important role in the turn of the plot. In this book, you will get to know some of them: Cordelia, the wilful daughter of King Lear; Emilia, a maid, but also the first feminist on stage; and first of all, a woman with devilish powers: Lady Macbeth. For a large part, she was the embodiment of evil. Shamelessly, she turned her husband into a murderer. Mr. and Mrs. Macbeth consequently flouted an important leadership lesson of Shakespeare: ambition without morality always takes a wrong turn. As did the Macbeth couple.

*If three witches predict that you will become king, then the sooner the better. At least, according to Macbeth. After all, his wife really, really, really desperately wants to be queen. Lady Macbeth convinces her husband to* kill the present king to speed things up a little. He does it, but suffers from a panic attack because he lacks the balls his wife has. She finds a way to turn others as the main suspects of the murder. However, some people at court think the case is rotten. The Macbeths kill these people, one by one, and with every murder their lunacy reaches a new height. A new visit to the witches makes him feel more at ease. As long as no trees of the forest march towards his castle, nothing is going to happen to them. They also assure him that he cannot be killed by anyone born of a woman. Pride comes before the fall, whether you are a royal couple or not. A sense of guilt is eating Lady Macbeth. She talks in her sleep and consequently reveals their secret. An army using branches and bushes as camouflage marches to Macbeth's Castle. The prediction of the witches comes true. Even Macbeth will be a victim now. He dies by the hand of a man born by a caesarean section. Shakespeare knows how to end a play. If necessary, by means of witchcraft.

## UNSEX ME, BABY!

Especially in *Macbeth*, Shakespeare plays with the overflow of male qualities in women and vice versa.

This is sometimes called 'unsexed'. This is about letting go of the feminine attributes in order to achieve (political) gain. In the 17th century, political power was reserved exclusively for men, unless, of course, you were Elizabeth I.

Lady Macbeth felt she was the strongest in the relationship with her husband and their success depended on her. Her definition of success being to get Macbeth on the throne as quickly as possible. She called for help: "Come you spirits that tend on mortal thoughts, unsex me here and fill me from the crown to the toe top-full of direst cruelty." In Macbeth's time, vigour was the same as cruelty – something Lady Macbeth had no problem whatsoever trading in exchange for her femininity. Shakespeare 'unsexes' Lady Macbeth, consciously giving her male attributes to enhance the credibility of her character to the audience.

And Macbeth himself? Is this man also 'unsexed' by the great writer? Yes, indeed. At the beginning of the play, Macbeth saw this coming when he replied to some of his rivals: "Ay, in the catalogue ye go for men, as hounds and greyhounds, mongrels, spaniels, curs." Macbeth knows and feels that men, like women, assume multiple identities and that he too will not be able to escape from that. As Lady Macbeth gains power, Macbeth's integrity and masculinity is increasingly questioned. And with that, his identity changes. From sheepdog to poodle as it were. His lack of courage makes him vulnerable to his wife's humiliating insults: "My hands are of your colour, but I shame to wear a heart so white." Ouch! That hurts!

## I HAVE A MAN'S MIND BUT A WOMAN'S MIGHT

Like Lady Macbeth, Elizabeth I must have male attributes to survive and to be considered competent for the responsibilities she has. Even though she is a queen with a fair amount of guts and shows some balls in what she does, she remains a woman in the eyes of the men around her, having to face all the prejudices that come into play. Being a woman (or for men: having feminine characteristics) did not help in obtaining a powerful position in society until far into to the 20th century. Four hundred years after Shakespeare and the strong leader Elizabeth I, it is still inconceivable for some people that a woman is to be a leader, let alone that she should lead a 'male' institute. For a long time, women were forced to 'unsex' themselves to be credible and get a good position in an organisation.

But in the 21st century, 'unsexing' is increasingly unnecessary. Women do not need to take on male attributes to be credible. And for men, this applies just as well. Female leaders no longer need to dress in chalk striped pants, and men sometimes dare to put their grey or dark blue uniform (also confused with a suit) in the closet in exchange for something more casual. The consensus is that good leadership contains both female and male elements. In most organisations, 'female' attributes such as empathy, loyalty, and care weigh in to 'male' attributes such as power, risk willingness and result orientation. There is a good mix between female and male qualities. Ideally, constitute a substantial minority or majority in an organisation. Like this, it is possible for them to decide on their own style of working and dealing with each other without adapting to the dominant masculine culture. In organisations rich in gender diversity, you generally see more and often better mutual cooperation and decision making, less difference in pay, and more attention to authenticity.

## MAVERICKS

The English language has a wonderful word for outsiders: 'mavericks' - named after Samuel Maverick, an American farmer who refused to brand his cows. He thought the procedure was cruel, but at the same time he knew how to take advantage of the incident, because he considered every cow without brand as his property. Mavericks are unconventional, a little rebellious, and are able to set an organisation in motion. They are creative, give momentum to innovation and are able to change the direction of an organisation with their ideas and energy. Mavericks do not need a brand mark. You recognise them by their attitude and behaviour.

I have a weak spot for mavericks, for the brilliant software developers who, on a diet of Luckies, Coke, and peanut butter and jelly sandwiches, spend their days in their own office. They will completely ignore you even if you are right in front of them because, for them, focus is everything. No rules apply to them because otherwise they would walk out the door never to come back. For the corporacte counsel, the thorn in the organisation's flesh. Haughty, dressed like a dandy, and with a remarkably sharp mind, this is the only person the secretary does not try to stop from entering the CEO's office without an appointment. Integrity is everything for them and they know how to balance the interests of the organisation and its values into perfection. Or the management consultant whose hobbies are caring for his koi carp and bodybuilding, sustaining a self-image that will surely be a feast to the eyes and ears of psychologists. Mavericks come in different shapes and forms but some traits are common. Outspoken, without any patience for stupidity (and you are judged to be stupid quite quickly), they are creative and innovative but above all authentic.

## CREATIVE MAVERICKS

John Sculley. The name sounds like a character from a Shakespeare play, but he is not. He entered the history books as the man who fired Steve Jobs from

Apple. The company is unprecedentedly successful and business is booming. Innovation and product development are paramount but other priorities, such as finance and marketing, are lost out of sight. Jobs is a strange guy in the eyes of the board of directors. They find it difficult to cope with his unpredictable and at times foolish behaviour and cannot keep track with his creative brain. They get Sculley, a seasoned 'traditional' manager, to fix things. He fires Jobs and as a consequence, Apple slowly starts rotting. Sculley's lack of appreciation for diversity in the company, his focus on marketing, but more in particular his total lack of feel for the Apple brand and the products that it should be producing, will eventually cost him his job. Apple hits rock bottom. After Sculley has disappeared in the coils, Apple buys the company that Jobs has set up after his departure. He himself makes a triumphant return as CEO. Later he will say that the departure at Apple inspired him to do some of his greatest innovations. His famous words about this are striking for creativity and innovation: 'Stay hungry. Stay foolish'.

## PROBLEM SOLVING SKILLS

Creativity is necessary when you are on stage. The space itself, the actors, the set decor and the play all have limitations and yet the audience wants to see something they can believe in. The creativity of the director, actors and the imagination of the public is called upon. In a play, it often revolves around a problem that arises and needs to be solved. Creative and innovative characters play a key role and provide solutions without which a play would take forever. These characters are a source of inspiration for their environment because they usually work with others to find and consequently give direction to the play. This makes them more successful than the solo player. In Act 1, King Henry is exemplary of success-ful but above all inspiring leadership.

*Henry looks around him at what, not so much later, would be remembered as the famous battlefield of Agin-court. It is cold, here and there fires are still burning, and he sees his soldiers stuck deep in the mud. They have had little food over the last few weeks and are hungry enough to end their campaign in France. That does not mean that they want to be slaughtered by the French who have taken camp on top of the hills before them with an overwhelmingly great army. Henry feels the responsibility and knows that he has to come up with something brilliant for him and his army to stay alive. As he squelches through the mud and lends his ear to his soldiers, a cunning plan unfolds in his head. With a little luck, it should work. And luck is what Henry and his men need. They need it badly.*

## HENRY HAS A PROBLEM

You could say that. For each English soldier ready to fight, the French have five soldiers on top of the hill. The solution that Henry has come up with is literally and figuratively a matter of life and death and he does not have much time left. Henry has to find a way to beat the French. He listens carefully to his soldiers, not just to get a sense of morale but also for inspiration. He then retires to overthink his options in solitude. He needs to rest in order to get his mind made up and to come up with a plan that will give his men both confidence as well as a good chance of victory. And suddenly, there it is: the solution.

The French troops are on top of a hill, a place over which they consider to have a competitive advantage. The English troops are in the valley and are protected by thousands of poles with a sharp point that the soldiers have hidden into the muddy ground. Sometimes you need some luck to make a plan work. Not only the muddy soil is advantageous to the English, but especially the attitude of the French: arrogant and convinced of being victorious. They're too impatient to wait for the English to make the first move, so, without hesitation, they initiate the attack. Mounted on their horses, the French run straight into the English ambush. They get stuck in the mud and become an easy prey for the English archers. No French rooster crows victory. Henry's plan has worked.

## A CHICKEN

Four phases can be distinguished in the creative process. If a problem arises, you start thinking about possible solutions. With the right people on board there are ideas about possible solutions that you can put into practice. This is the breeding phase. In the third phase, the best solution is to overcome the problem that will surface, and in the final phase you will investigate whether the solution found will actually yield the much-needed result. These stages are also reflected in the problems that Shakespeare must solve for Henry.

PREPARATION ⟩ INCUBATION ⟩ ILLUMINATION ⟩ VERIFICATION ⟩

*Figure 4. The four phases of problem solving (Wallas)*

Organisations often make the same mistakes: the importance of the first two phases is underestimated. Thinking and breeding are very important to gain a good insight into the problem you want to solve. Understanding the breeding phase is often forgotten, particularly the peace and quiet you need to breed. Breeding in a hectic environment often does not deliver the results you get when there's time to consider different alternatives. This demonstrates the importance of giving the creative maverick the time and space to tackle problems. Patience is key so you should never disturb a breeding chicken. Once the solution has been found, it must be tested. Just as an egg can be prepared in different ways, the solution can sometimes be applied differently. You don't like it boiled? Then try frying it.

Is there actually a problem? That is the main question that should be considered in the first instance. Remember the Apple Pippen? It was a game console and Apple's response to the dominance of Nintendo and PlayStation. Apple considered it a problem that they did not make game computers. In the end, only 40,000 were sold worldwide, because the consumer simply did not want it. The consumer did not see Apple's problem because there were alternatives from which to choose. Not all that Apple touches turns to gold.

People make the same mistake. For example, if you are dissatisfied with your job, you can look for another employer. But if you find out in your new job that you are actually dissatisfied with the work you do, then this is not a solution to your problem. To think and to breed. Don't get off to a false start.

## INNOVATIVE MAVERICK

Many organisations tend to hire people who 'fit into' the organisation and consequently do not differ too much from the norm. They look for people with whom the colleagues can easily get along. However, it is also important to hire people who at first glance do not fit so well. Without friction, there is no shine. For example, after becoming a legend in his own country in Northern Africa, Othello gets an opportunity to shine in Venice. By appointing him, the rulers in that city take a chance that eventually ended badly because he literally does not know how to survive in the organisation. Before his death, he makes some nice wins, but that is of little comfort to him.

*Othello is a soldier. A general to be precise. He fought long and hard to get that position. He builds up his reputation with his unconventional ideas about warfare, which lead the rich city of Venice to recruit him from Africa to Europe. Because of his appearance, Othello is an outsider in the city where he lives and works. His ideas and strategy deviate from the common thoughts of warfare in Europe. Coming from another continent and having grown up with different values from the society he is part of as a general of the Venetian army, he struggles with expectations and suspicions of his environment. At the same time, he realises that because he is an outsider he can do things that others cannot. In the end, Othello goes down. He underestimates the informal relationships that are not visible to him and which he cannot feel.*

## OTHELLO KNOWS BEST

Othello was a maverick in several respects. He is a dark-skinned foreigner in a completely lily-white environment. He is unfamiliar with the standards and values of the organisation for which he works. In addition, he is also of age and married to a white woman who could be his daughter. All of these factors affect Othello's position in Venice and in the army. What the people of Venice fail to do is to guide him well in his new environment, to make him familiar with the most important values so that he can adapt, be successful and can survive.

The Venetian army lured him to Italy because of his reputation. He has knowledge and skills that are not present in Venice itself. Othello learned to fight on another continent, with other soldiers and weapons against other enemies. He is successful and the Venetians want to benefit from it. With him in their midst, they expect to innovate their way of warfare by learning from his insights and making use of his experience. Othello's vision of warfare has far-reaching consequences and sets new demands for its officers. Brute power and courage are no longer that important. Now it's the mathematical insight to accurately hit the target with the canons that prevails.

## HELLO STRANGER

Othello is at the heart of innovation. He has the courage to say farewell to the things we know and trust. His unique background generates a wave of creativity. That is the first start to innovation. This is what innovation is about: changes in systems or processes. You add new features or new functions. It can also mean using existing functions differently. All innovations start with creative ideas and are a logical consequence of the previously followed creative process. In fact, without creativity, there is no innovation. Any organisation that wants to innovate must give space to creativity.

Venice knows that if it wants to be successful, it is important to keep creativity and new insights flowing so that innovations strengthen its competitiveness. Under the guidance of Othello, Venice seeks new and more efficient ways of conquering a new city or sinking a ship. That saves money and, at that time, a lot of human life. The city is able to embrace diversity, to look beyond what is known and is therefore more successful than all the states around it. The only thing that still needs work is the induction program.

## AUTHENTIC MAVERICK

What is authentic? When you look in the dictionary, you will find definitions such as 'reliable', 'genuine' and 'credible'. An aphorism on a poster would state: 'Be yourself there are so many others' and a philosopher would ask you: 'Who are you without the idea that you have to impress others?' In any case, authenticity has nothing to do with having only one face in an organisation. In different situations, you have different faces. By being authentic you show a thin red line, a thread in your behaviour: you never compromise the real you. Authentic people are important for the diversity of an organisation. Authentic people often deviate from the norm and sometimes they struggle to find their way around in an organisation. Consequently, the organisation is challenged to deal with them. For example, the Danish court has trouble with the authenticity of Hamlet who has been acting a bit strange lately.

*Hamlet is not doing well. You would not feel well either if an uncle killed your father and married your mother only three weeks later, if friends betrayed you, and a ghost haunted you at night. The ghost tells Hamlet his uncle is his father's murderer and Hamlet vows to take revenge. But how to make a murderer? Hamlet is a bit of a philosopher and as such he is constantly in doubt about what actions to take: 'To be or not to be,' you know it well. He is unsure if he can trust and believe the ghost and does not know what to do. In the end he decides to pretend he has gone insane to make it easier to investigate the truth. Naturally, there is a girl at stake as well and some believe he is crazy about her. Quite professionally, he manages to trap his uncle and prove he is the killer. Because in the meantime Hamlet travelled to England, had an encounter with pirates, fought in a duel, accidently offered his mother poisoned wine and stabbed his uncle before eventually dying himself, this is Shakespeare's longest play.*

## AWAY WITH THE FAIRIES

Halfway through the play, Hamlet's uncle sends him off on a cruise from Denmark to England with two old college friends supposedly because some fresh air will do him well. But behind his good intentions, he is plotting a conspiracy with these so-called friends of Hamlet to murder him. When his friends start questioning him on open sea, Hamlet senses he is in peril and knows he cannot trust his friends any longer.

A wonderful confrontation follows when Hamlet asks one of his friends to play the pipe, which, according to him, is just as easy as lying. When his friend says he cannot play the pipe, Hamlet confronts him: "Why, look you know, how unworthy a thing you make of me! You would play upon me; you would seem to know my stops, you would pluck out the heart of mystery, you would sound me from my lowest note to the top of my compass, and there is much music, excellent voice in this little organ, yet cannot you make it speak. Why, do you think that I am easier to be played on than a pipe? Call me what instrument you will, though you can fret me, you cannot play upon me. God bless you sir!"

## HELP!

Hamlet is depressed and that is only normal after all the unfortunate events he goes through. Someone with depression must be but themselves to get out of that deep black hole. Hamlet wants to be sure that people are not going to betray him, ridicule or otherwise take control of him. But he feels threatened now that he no longer can sincerely trust his own friends. He can no longer be himself.

For employees or colleagues with a depression or burnout trust is also of great importance. This might be trust in the therapist helping them to get back to work again; or trust in the manager and colleagues when they return to work for the first time; trust in the organisation that it still has faith in them. Hamlet is an example of psychic diversity in an organisation. Hamlet-type of employees need someone they trust and who is willing to make decisions for them from time to time.

## THE BIRD IS KNOWN BY ITS NOTE, A MAN BY HIS WORD

In most organisations, psychic diversity is invisible simply because employees do not like to disclose any information regarding their mental health. As a result, every organisation ends up employing people with mental disorders. Sometimes is this a deliberate choice, but usually the employer is not aware of the circumstances. Such disorders may be temporary or more permanent. Sometimes employees will be open about it, but more often than not, they will prefer to keep it to themselves.

Some organisations make conscious use of psychic diversity. One example might be a software company that likes working with people with Asperger's syndrome, whose competences may actually be well suited to the work of the organisation. These include attention to detail, analytical ability, and orderly work. The idea of psychic diversity on the work floor is not such a crazy one in the end. However, it does come with its pros and cons. Mental disorders are associated with stigmas, such as aggressive behaviour, poor cooperation, and limited social skills. These prejudices urgently need to be challenged and tackled.

Proper support and coaching with the team is important in order to keep a good cooperation and to ensure that the maverick does not become an outsider. Chances are you work with colleagues who have a mental disorder. Many will not be open about it because of fear of negative reactions and discrimination.

## AUTHENTICITY ON THE WORK FLOOR

Authentic people are not afraid to voice their opinion, even if it does not align with their manager or colleagues. They are driven by inner motives instead of being guided by what is happening around them. They are confident of their talents and not afraid to show them to others. Personal and professional growth are important as well as good and personal contacts. They will try to avoid prejudice about others as much as possible, but do not succeed all the time.

## SCENE 4

(A random kitchen in a random restaurant. Two waiters are polishing the cutlery in a quiet corner.)

**Waiter**: (whispering). Say, have you seen chef Thomas getting out of control this evening?

**The other waiter**: No need to whisper, he's already gone home. But yes, he put on quite a show again. Haven't seen him this mad in ages.

**Waiter**: What happened? I heard he sucker punched a guest?

**The other waiter**: Well, he was close if it wasn't for Maurice who stopped him in the hallway as chef was about to enter the restaurant.

**Waiter**: Let me take a wild guess: the guest had something to say about the food?

**The other waiter**: Duh-uh, that was easy. A venison tenderloin came back. He wanted it well done.

**Waiter**: Whoa, yep, then you are looking for trouble. But if you want your meat well done, why not go to the shitty McDonalds?

**The other waiter**: Exactly the point chef Thomas was making however he was using the F word. He slammed his pan on the stove, threw in the venison and wanted to go into the restaurant to serve it in person.

**Waiter**: In person as in 'here's your well-done filet mignon and never come back, you culinary barbarian' or something like that?

**The other waiter**: He was out of his mind, so yes, that would probably have happened if it wasn't for Maurice.

**Waiter**: Free fighting a nutty chef, that's also a restaurant manager's job.

If you feel you have the space to be yourself, you are less stressed and generally happy and satisfied with your work. Unless you work alone, this is easier said than done. As soon as you interact with other people, like the guests in your restaurant, it can be difficult. You will not get along equally easily with all colleagues and people around you. You will find some are annoying, others you really do not understand and that will affect you anyway. Sticking to your authentic character is a challenge.

Authenticity is crucial to staying healthy. It is a paradox that this is important for employees who are ill or disabled. Being true to yourself is important whether you have a visible disability or a mental disorder. Not every employee is equally open about disability, illness or disorder. And certainly, not everything is visible. An organisation where you can and may be authentic is a safe environment. It avoids stress and ensures a good balance between work and personal life. This is good for every employee with or without mental disorder, sick or healthy. Let's face it, at work, anyone can lose it from time to time.

## THOSE DAMN MAVERICKS

Mavericks colour an organisation, boost creativity and innovation, and determine the degree of authenticity. They let an organisation grow and flourish and bring about a natural balance. Nevertheless, sometimes they drive you crazy. They are not the easiest colleagues to deal with and they are certainly not easy on themselves either. Mavericks have difficulty finding their way around an organisation. They struggle with their authenticity and the expectations of an organisation. They often take as much energy as they give and that challenges managers. An organisation will benefit from giving them a safe place to work and, above all, trust, a lot of trust. They are demanding but you will get your return on investment. Especially if you allow them to be who they are.

In authentic organisations, employees get trust and freedom. These organisations prevent creative ideas from dying prematurely by a hasty and not well thought through judgment of others. You are well stocked on compliments to increase engagement and there are two enthusiastic thumbs up for cooperation. Authentic organisations do not undermine their employees in public. Mavericks will be demotivated if they are being scrutinised in front of their colleagues and any good ideas coming from them after that are limited. They appreciate honest feedback: just say it. Mavericks believe that they are either nothing or nerds until proven the contrary. Their role models are the Wright brothers and their first prototype aircraft, Edison, Tesla, Gates, Ford - to name just a few true mavericks.

Hamlet, finally, acts like he's gone mad. The play is not very explicit on that. In any case, this maverick is no longer in motion due to the circumstances. The dilemmas he is confronted with are simply too big: nobody is there to help him, he does not trust anyone anymore and that has disastrous consequences. His doubts start with the most famous sentence of all times:

*"To be or not to be, that is the question:*
*Whether 'tis nobler in the mind to suffer*
*The slings and arrows of outrageous fortune*
*Or to take arms against a sea of troubles and by opposing end them*
*To die, to sleep."*

Inaction is poisonous. It makes you unable to judge the other and it will cause you to lose control over the outcome. This applies to everyone: leader, manager and employee. Take action. Help the Hamlets around you.

## DIVERSE TEAMS

Men and women, mavericks, philosophers, hunters and lobbyists: every organisation and most teams are more or less diverse. It is simply about what you want to see and, most importantly, if you can see through what is invisible. The composition of teams and the diversity you are looking for depends on the work that needs to be done and the people who have to do that. Some organisations benefit from mostly homogeneous teams, while others need more diversity to be successful.

People feel comfortable in an environment where there are shared professional values and where colleagues share the same attitude towards work. It does not matter what they look like or where they come from. Shared values are a bridge between different cultures and backgrounds. There are plenty of examples of teams where solely the professional relationship counts. In these cases, your knowledge is more important than who you are. Discussions are limited to work and the colleagues share the belief that silence is golden when it comes to their personal life. Work is work. Home is home. That is their shared value: what happens at home stays at home and is none of their co-workers' business. An example of this are construction workers. They often work together in multicultural teams and if someone in the team works just as hard as the remaining colleagues, there is a connection. The fact that you are a construction worker is more important than where you come from and what you eat in the afternoon. Although they all look different and have a diverse background, this is a homogeneous team rather than a diverse team.

## WE ARE LIKE EACH OTHER (AREN'T WE?)

Within homogeneous groups there are unwritten rules of great importance. In such a team, a different vision can be seen as a threat. Suppose the construction workers are told by their supervisor to wear pink jeans. Chances are that they could see it as a threat to their image and that can lead to conflicts. A new way of working can initially lead to resistance as well. After all, we have always done it that way, so why change? In a group that is too close, group thinking can occur over the years and that may pose a real danger. A close group can put pressure on an individual to go along with the general opinion in an attempt to silence any criticism against the group's vision. That leads to good professionals being easily influenced into taking poorer group decisions.

To avoid these negative effects of diversity, some organisations have a preference for teams with equal values and attitudes towards work. For example, relatively simple work, or work that is seen as typically male (construction, engineering) or female (nursing). It explains why some organisations are less accessible to, for example, women, people with disabilities, non-qualified graduates, or people from other cultural backgrounds. In this case, group formation is taken for granted. "If it be man's work, I'll do it," says one of Henry's soldiers. And that is still the case in some work places.

## WE ARE NOT LIKE EACH OTHER (OR ARE WE?)

Some organisations rely heavily on creativity and innovation to achieve results. If an organisation is creative, it is able to innovate, break through fixed thinking patterns and thereby increasing its competitiveness. Henry shows that you need imagination to be creative and solve problems. So, you need some creative Henry-types in your team but not too many because you also need people who test the ideas, implement them, and bring them to the finish line. Everyone has their own unique talents and it is for that reason that diversity is so important. A diverse team knows more because of the different backgrounds of its members. There are different visions that enable them to make better deliberations and to think of different alternatives to the problem. With the difference in knowledge and experience, they are able to identify errors faster and expose important information because of a broader perspective.

For example, a software development team needs different skills to make a successful product. The idea is as important as the execution and testing is particularly relevant: what good is an idea if it doesn't work? Advertising professionals do not benefit only from creative minds. They also need people who can shape and execute the wild ideas. A restaurant needs a good cook with creative ideas, but also waiters who know how to serve guests.

In order for creativity to flourish, it is important that there is time and space to think and breed. For example, at Google, employees get 20% of their time to do just this and this time can also be used to get to know colleagues better. The more information is shared, the more obvious it will become where the consensus and differences are. This has a positive effect on team efficiency and eliminates existing prejudices.

Managers have an important role to play. A good manager understands how to challenge employees to be more open about who they are in order to strengthen the team's spirit and boost individual talent. Ultimately, this creates the much-needed trust and the confidence that are key to achieving team results. In a diverse team, you need to be able to express yourself safely so that problems are quickly overcome and change is possible. If not, group thinking will prevail, killing all forms of creativity with the almighty argument: 'we have always done it this way.'

There are risks associated with creating a diverse organisation. For example, there may not be enough time and attention provided to the cultural change.

Perhaps the organisation is not ready to cope with conflicts that arise amongst people with different characters or of different backgrounds. There may be discrimination and bullying or communication problems amongst people who do not look alike and have different standards and values. These risks do not counteract the risk of loss of competitiveness. The late Dutch football player and coach Johan Cruyff left just as many great memories of his tactics as of his personal wisdom. He once said: 'every disadvantage has its advantage.' And this could not be more true.

## DIVERSITY IS LOAM

What we don't know, we fear. And that is the main pitfall when it comes to diversity. We like to be with people who look like us, and if that is not the case, then prejudices arise, hindering the cooperation in a team. Think of the young person who believes older people do not want to change anymore. Think of the woman who is wondering if the man on the other side of the table gets paid more for the same job. Imagine the western businessman who is sure that his Chinese client wants to eat Chinese in the evening, burps and wants to sing in a karaoke bar. As people work together for a longer period of time, they get to know each other better, putting prejudices aside and increasing the level of efficiency in their teamwork. It should be said, though, that none of this has anything to do with looking alike, but with shared values. The working mentality of the elderly, the female desire to be equal, and the awkward way we want to make someone feel at home.

On stage, diversity is very visible and heavily accentuated to make the characters come to life. Writer and director make full use of this trick to provide the play with substance, speed, and power. Some characters are agile, others extremely closed. They accept or ignore each other. There are fights and tears, laughter and betrayal. They are accepted into a group or banished from it. They work together, invent new plans or counteract each other. Wherever one is welcome, the other will be banned (if it is equally true). On stage, these processes unfold as fast as lightning. On the work floor, they take place in a delayed form. Diversity is the fertile ground in which employees grow. It's a safe environment that uses everyone's unique qualities and talents. It motivates them and increases engagement. A manager must fertilise the soil with a good sense of relationships, ability to cope with conflicts and attention to norms and values. It is easier to manage a homogeneous team where you do not have to worry about many different characters, each with their own strengths and weaknesses. On the other hand, a football team consisting solely of defenders will have difficulty scoring. Establishing diversity is primarily a fight against prejudices. The power of diversity is to discover similarities in the differences.

And what about you? How do you feel about diversity? Do you use it or are you being used? Do you feel you have the space in your organisation to be yourself or must you look for who you really are at the end of each working day? Do you know who are the mavericks in your organisation? Who dares to be different? Or perhaps you are an outsider yourself?

ACT 3

**PROMPTER**

OR **SABOTEUR?**

*"Who so firm that cannot be seduced?"*

*Julius Caesar*

In the seventeenth century, masses of people came to The Globe, Shakespeare's theatre in London, to be entertained for an afternoon. In terms of atmosphere the theatre was like a football stadium today. There was no concern for etiquette; it was packed with rowdy and often very drunk people. The theatre was a very popular form of entertainment at that time. The Londoners stood or sat in the theatre the same way we watch a soap opera on the television in the evening. Just like with soaps today, there used to be a new play almost every day. The crowd craved for the eventful activities on stage full of guile and deceit. These are not so different from the daily intrigues at work. Guile and deception are an almost natural pheno-menon in organisations. But while obvious, they are just as much undesirable on the work floor. Sharing sensitive information with the competitor about your organisation makes you a traitor. Misleading a colleague so that he gets a reprimand makes you a deceiver. Both are recognisable and the conflicts that arise must be solved. To prevent guile and deceit one must diligently manage the norms and values of an organisation and nurture integrity.

Guile and deceit are the poison in this act. Norms, values and integrity are the antidote. This act is first and foremost about the most famous treason in his-tory: the murder of Julius Caesar. How do you recog-nise a traitor and what other shady characters can be found in your surroundings? Next, I also describe how Othello is betrayed by a faithful adjutant who has been deceived. The values of the organisation are the roots of integrity. Cordelia, the daughter of King Lear, plays the leading role.

Shakespeare uses betrayal, fraud, values and inte-grity to ask his audience questions while at the same time questioning social issues. When is it okay to cheat on someone? When not? What if a difference of insight arises within the leadership of an organisation? Can you sail on different moral compasses? Shakespeare shows that personal values and integrity are inextricably linked.

## BETRAYAL

Caesar is betrayed by Brutus. It is betrayal in its purest form: not being loyal to his emperor. It is not surprising that the traitor Brutus is eventually deceived himself and gets a knife in his back. The karma of Shakespeare's characters is not always that strong. For the emperor himself it was too little too late. Revenge is sweet except for the dead.

Betrayal is drama and deceit is everlasting. Shakespeare uses it in different ways and not just in an evil manner. Sometimes deceit derives from love; sometimes from self-protection or pure opportunism; sometimes as a joke. He shows that betrayal and deceit can be functional or even acceptable because they are necessary to keep an organisation on track. While Shakespeare describes love and lust in a suggestive way, he is very concrete when it comes to betrayal, integrity and manipulation. "And you, Brutus?" are the famous words that Julius Caesar utters when he gets stabbed by his friend Brutus. To this day, people are still surprised by the 'betrayal' of a 'reliable' colleague. Brutus was a colleague, even a friend of Caesar, but he conceived himself as a traitor for personal gain only - one of the main motives for betrayal. It can happen to anyone, including you.

*Your first encounter with Julius Caesar was probably via Asterix and Obelix. You may not even know that Shakespeare wrote a play about him. The character of Caesar in the comic is just as well depicted as what Shakespeare has to say about this Roman emperor.*
*Julius has the dubious honour of being the first dictator in history. In Roman times, that is not really a big thing, and after all his victories, he deserves it. A fortune-teller (nowadays it's Twitter) tells him to watch his back during an upcoming holiday because otherwise there may not be too much left to celebrate. Others also have a premonition and urge him not to go to the Senate to attend the celebration. Caesar ignores the advice, closes his 'twitter account', and goes out to enjoy his power and the adoration of the Romans. Meanwhile, Brutus,*

*one of his most loyal followers, is manipulated. Opponents of Caesar convince him that he should be emperor because Caesar is far too ambitious and hungered for more power. They stage a coup and Brutus takes over the reign - though not for long. The loyal soldier, Marcus Antonius, together with the son of Caesar, manages to unleash a revolt that will eventually cost Brutus and his co-conspirators their lives. It is an 'eye for an eye, a tooth for a tooth' - a typical way to die in a Shakespeare play.*

## BETRAY THE BETRAYOR

What cost Caesar his life was not so much his ambition and hunger for power, but the lack of trust in his surroundings. Narcissism and blind spots are always near for anyone in a powerful position. That's because being blinded by power involves risks. Caesar not only ignores the fortune-teller's advice but also the urgent requests of his wife and his most faithful advisors to stay safely at home. Trusting your environment is essential to survival in an organisation, whether you are a leader, manager or employee.

Confidence at the top is however shaky and the motto of many modern-day dictators (I would almost write: CEOs) may well be: 'trust is good but control is better.' They borrow these words from Lenin, a Roman-style Russian dictator, who learned from Caesar's teachings and his fate. Control might very well be the reason why Lenin, unlike Caesar, was fortunate enough to die peacefully. Trust and control are at odds with each other: control undermines the feeling that your employer trusts you.

Trust is an important value in collaboration. You want to be able to trust your colleagues especially in jobs like those performed by firefighters, surgeons or construction workers. It is good to know that you can really trust the majority of your colleagues - people with whom you do not have to be cautious, who share mutual respect, and with whom you would walk through fire. In these environments, your colleagues will be checking your work but not you. And that is an important nuance.

# SCENE 5

(A meeting room in a random office building in a random city. The co-workers of a department are, unexpectedly, called into a meeting. The CEO is in front of the group. Next to him a VP. The atmosphere is tense.)

**CEO**: Let me get right to the point; I have made an executive decision to terminate your VP effective immediately.

(Long silence)

**CEO**: I have been dissatisfied with the performance of your department for a long time. I hold leadership responsible for that. Things have to change and the person standing next to me is not the right person to do so.

(An even longer silence)

**CEO**: Any questions? Otherwise I am going to attend to more important issues.

(Hubbub in the room)

**Co-worker**: Will you name a successor?

**CEO**: Only if I can find someone who does not provoke as much opposition as he does.

Betrayal and deceit are opposite of trust. They both come in many forms and are often unrecognizable. It is not as simple as someone who pulls out a knife in the open and stabs you in the back. It may well be a sign of civilisation that betrayal and deceit nowadays are generally executed in words and not with weapons. But as the previous scene illustrates, that does not, however, make it less painful.

## THE TRAITOR BETRAYED

One of the main leadership lessons of Shakespeare's in Act 1 is to not listen to gossip. Othello does, and that is a pity because he is doing quite well for himself. He has a nice job as a general in the Venetian Army and a lovely, albeit way too young, wife. Life is good.

*Othello is a Moor - a man of North-African origin as we would say today. He is a general with a high reputation in the service of the Venetian army: a mercenary, a military hero. Iago is his standard-bearer for many years, his confidant but also a sickly jealous psychopath. He is jealous of Othello about everything and everyone. First, he sets up Othello's father-in-law against him. Next, he stages a fight between two other confidants of Othello. Then he screws over his colleague Cassio by spreading lies about him. This is all done to flatter Othello with his fall as ultimate goal and taking his position as soon as the opportunity arises. Desdemona, the wife of the general, is the spindle in the story. Iago spins a web of lies claiming she cheated on Othello with half the city of Venice. He does this so convincingly that Othello kills his own wife. When Iago's deception is finally out in the open, Othello takes his own life.*

If you, like Othello, work in a new or unfamiliar environment, you may feel insecure about how people look at you. Particularly in the first couple of months of your employment or if you are on an assignment working abroad. For Othello, that is no different. This uncertainty makes him sensitive to the words of Iago, the devil's Plotter who feeds on gossip and who deceives him to believe his wife Desdemona is cheating on him. Othello does not bother to check the sources and fails to dig into the underlying motivation driving the rumours. He does not see the higher plan of Iago and takes action immediately - a lethal one that will kill both his wife and himself. The lesson? Do not let gossip take control of you without checking it and understanding the reason for it. If you fail to do that, you will harm the people around you. Actually, you will commit professional suicide because, like Othello, you will not get away with it.

## IT'S JUST AS EASY AS LYING

On the work floor, you will have colleagues who influence your self-esteem. Among them there will be Iagos trying to bring you down, consciously or unconsciously. This is not obvious or written on

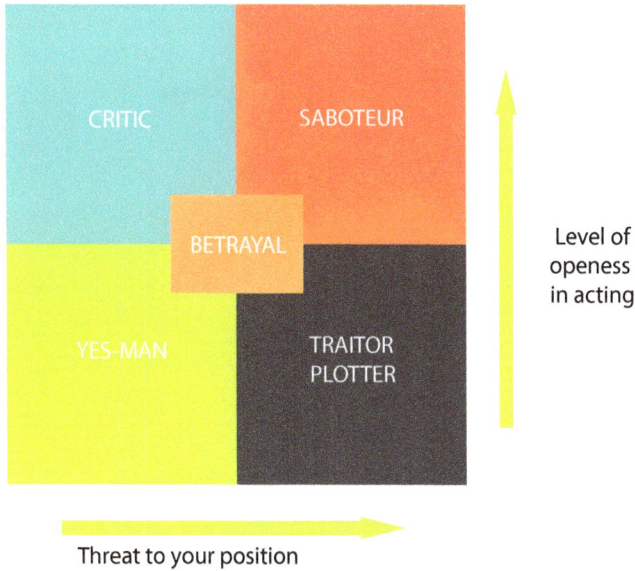

Figure 5. The five types of deceivers (Olivier)

their foreheads so you need your intuition and consciousness to recognise them. These colleagues can be dangerous for your position in the organisation and do not always act openly and honestly. There are five types to be distinguished: the Critic and the Yes-Man will influence your self-image but are not dangerous by definition. However, the Saboteur, the Plotter, and Traitor are.

## THE CRITIC AND THE YES-MAN

The Critic's comments and criticism are driven by a desire to resist change. They romanticise the past, are conservative and consequently cherish what is. The mirror they hold in front of you has two sides. One is a window on the past, while the other is looking to the future. This complexity can be a reason to ignore the Critic, but be careful not to do so. The feedback you receive from the critic is very direct and, as such, valuable. Their intention is usually positive but sometimes Critics have a terrible way of expressing it. Ignoring the Critics is risky. Not listening or disrespecting them can cause the Critics to become Saboteurs. Critics are loyal by nature and their criticism is an expression of appreciation, even though it sometimes does not feel that way. It is up to you to decide whether the criticism is right or not; whether the intention is to counteract change or that there is a core of truth when it comes to your performance.

The Yes-Man will constantly applaud you and the organisation, get coffee and support every idea. Of course it is nice to have someone like this around. Because that way there is always someone who does exactly what you say or what you want. But it can get very quiet with too many Yes-Men around you: they do not ask questions, show limited initiative and will keep any comments to themselves. With too many Yes-Men around, you run the risk of being blind to your own performance. Do not be mistaken, even Yes-Men can have a double agenda. Take Iago, for example. It seems like he is not dangerous to you at all because of his flattery, but, in the meantime, he undermines your position. Brutus is also a Yes-Man in the first instance. Until the moment he feels that Caesar no longer listens to him. From that moment on, he is open to the intrigues around him and it is only a matter of time for him to betray Caesar.

## THE SABOTEUR AND THE PLOTTER

You have to watch out for the Saboteur and the Plotter. They are a lot like each other, but the Saboteur tells you right to your face what they think of you while the Plotter gossips behind your back at the vending machine. For both, the glass is always half-empty and with this negative attitude they occupy the work floor. Every new idea they will behold with suspicion and will always first illuminate the bad sides. The Saboteur and the Plotter want the organisation to move forward, but almost by definition disagree with the direction it should take. The moment is not right, or the people who are going to do the work are not okay. The Saboteur and Plotter are only interested in the status quo. Do not allow them to influence your work or to be the dead horse that needs some proper flogging. Confront them with their behaviour ('Who? Me? Negative? No way!'). Let them know you are onto them. The Saboteur and the Plotter are the black holes of the organisation into which all energy disappears.

## THE TRAITOR

Traitors undermine you because they do not agree with the position you have or the work you do. The Traitor wants a change, definitely with negative consequences for you. Julius Caesar knows something is going on and that betrayal is on the verge. But because he stays in the denial phase for too long, this eventually costs him his life. Rarely is decisiveness more important than in this case.

If you have a Traitor in your midst you are in a nasty situation: it's either the Traitor or you. It is quite often as simple as that. It does not necessarily have to result in a difficult redundancy procedure. Traitors are also ambitious. Another position may well be the best option for all parties involved.

## SO: LOVE EVERYONE, TRUST A FEW, DO WRONG TO NONE

For actors, it is important to be aware of the intentions of their fellow actors. An intent is a resolution to do something and the only way to create a fascinating spectacle for the audience. Not all intentions are transformed into action, but they do clarify the behaviour that someone exhibits. At the workplace, colleagues seem to be less aware of the intentions of the people with whom they work. Despite old methods, such as work meetings, and modern methods, like scrum, colleagues often do not know what the others are doing, let alone why. The intention with which someone is doing their work and, above all, the reasons for someone to be working at all are often unknown. This is not just for the immediate colleagues but just as often for the manager.

It is important to be aware of the intentions of the people around you, whatever you do in an organisation or whatever position you hold. It explains the behaviour you see and experience. Take for example the sudden difficult relationship with the nice colleague next to you after your salary increase is higher than his. Jealousy and envy express themselves in behaviour that you encounter in every function and at every level. They are human emotions and your nice colleague is only human after all. It can help you to understand things that seem to be strange at first. It may even be good to name them. In any case, you give your colleagues the chance to be candid about their feelings. What is keeping you from having a cup of coffee with your colleague in order to talk about that salary increase? 'Say, it seems to me that our collaboration has been difficult lately. I think that is a pity. What do you think is happening?'

## VALUES

Betrayal and deceit always conflict with the current norms and values in an organisation, specifically those written down on paper or posted on the wall. Putting values in writing is one thing, let them determine your life and work is another. The financial crisis, the banks' values, and the behaviour of directors show that deceit does not always have to lead to raised eyebrows or disciplinary measures in every organisation. It does, however, put the integrity of an organisation on edge. Morality is sometimes far-fetched and Shakespeare certainly knew how to deal with that.

The norms and values in the seventeenth 17th century were highly dependent on one's social class. The theatre played a remarkable role in the connection between the classes because it is the only place where pauper and nobility, people from all social groups of the population come together. The norms to which the rich must adhere differed significantly from those of the poor. Their core values contrasted greatly. At the beginning of the twentieth century, you could still see that lack of shared norms and values in society and in organisations. There was no equality between men and women or between the worker and the office staff. Fortunately, today this has changed and, in most organisations, core values apply to everyone from C-suite to the blue-collar workers.

Many organisations post their values on a wall, have them as screensaver on computer screens or call them out and review them once a year at the Christmas party. Employees do not feel bound by the values because of this casual approach. These values are in their heads but not in the hearts and that makes it difficult to act upon them. The leaders in an organisation have the moral obligation to set an example for their colleagues when it comes to its norms and values. They must pave the way from the head to the heart: setting a good example to follow. These words are so true that even Shakespeare could have easily written them.

# SCENE 6

(A random corporate headquarters of a random multinational. Three managers are standing in front of the vending machine, talking about Charles, the CEO.)

**One manager**:  I spoke to Laura yesterday. You know, the one from legal and she told me she got a twenty percent raise from Charles.

**The other manager**: Really, you don't say. How many tears did that cost her?

**One manager**: (laughing) Knowing her? Probably not that many. You know how Charles is if it comes to crying women.

**The other manager**: It is rather odd, isn't it? The man is so talented, has achieved so much and then he does something like this.

**One manager**: Well, put a woman in heels in front of him and there is not that much left. Or he must hide behind that ridiculously large desk of his.

(both laugh impudently)

**The other manager**: So, Laura did not feel embarrassed at all to share this with you? Sobbing in front of the boss to get a raise?

**One manager**: No, not at all, she even seemed proud of it.
**The other manager**: Can we pull that off as well, you reckon?
**One manager**: Ha! What do you think?

Values are aimed at guiding organisations through good and bad time by clarifying what the organisation stands for in the longer term. Core values are important for any organisation because they are a reflection of the vision and the reason for existence. They give employees support, inspiration and, more importantly, they determine attitude and behaviour. At least, that is the theory. It certainly does not happen everywhere and leaders, particularly behind closed doors, struggle to show exemplary behaviour, as we saw in the previous scene. Despite good intentions, putting words into action may be a challenge in practice.

## ARE YOU A JERK?

What if you do not meet the standards and values of an organisation? Are you a Traitor? A Jerk? Not per se, but you do find yourself on an inclined plane, because it depends solely on what the core values in your organisation are. If a critical observation is a core value, the Yes-Men find themselves also on that same inclined plane. It is important for employees to be able to identify themselves with the norms and values of their employer. It means you feel at home and that your organisation enables you to get the best out of yourself. Human beings and organisations change. Behaviours change and so do goals. Therefore, not every colleague will continue to comply with the norms and values of the organisation over the years. You will probably see them around you too. Colleagues looking for the limits of what is permissible or sometimes passing over those same limits. There can be friction between the norms and values and the way someone does their work. It can also add some extra shine to it. Who is the Jerk in an organisation and who is the Star?

The proverbial Jerk is the colleague who performs well but willingly ignores the norms and values of the organisation. Because of their excellent performance, Jerks often get away with it. Particularly in the first years when the organisation and the

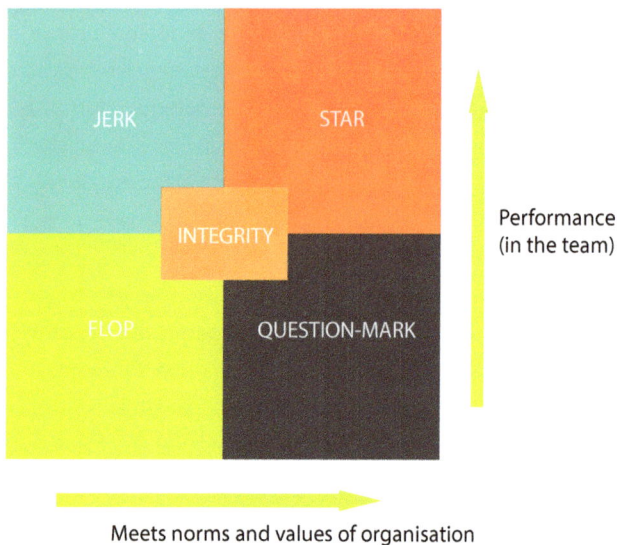

Figure 6. The Values Performance Matrix (Welch)

colleagues are getting to know them. The performance of the Star is great too, but the Star meets and exceeds the norms and values of the organisation. The Question Mark is the colleague we all love: social, kind, and fond of the work and colleagues. Even though the performance of Question-Marks leaves quite a bit to be desired, a manager will find it difficult to address the issue with them because they are genuinely nice. The organisation needs to part ways as quickly as possible with any Flops in the work floor. If someone does not meet the norms and values of the organisation and is an underperformer, wouldn't it be better if they worked somewhere else?

## ARCHETYPES IN A BOX

The Careerist, Philosopher and other archetypes in Act 1 of this book move through the above quadrant. Some will eventually come to a halt somewhere.
Fans are often Stars because of their dedication. A lack of appreciation however can cause Fans to question themselves and the organisation. The darling Fan will always advocate the norms and values, together with the Philosopher who is pure in the doctrine. Philosophers are often Stars but can become Question-Marks in times of great change. The Careerists will be seen as Stars by the organisation because of the results they bring. At least at first, that is. Once it becomes clear how these results are achieved and how Careerists make a mockery of an organisation's norms and values, they will be exposed as the Jerks

they really are. If organisations address this negative behaviour, some Careerist will become shining Stars, while others will leave the club. The Lobbyist is the only one moving rapidly through all four quadrants. This makes perfect sense since Lobbyists will use every corner of the quadrant if that is in their best interest. The Lobbyist is therefore the most difficult one to manage of all archetypes. The Parent is, of course, a Star – or so they think so. In a team, due to their status, Parents are difficult to manage and they are often on the verge between Stars and Question-Marks. A performance review, let alone an exit meeting, will always come as a surprise.

Despite the fact that eighty percent of the employees believe they belong to the top twenty percent of the organisation, you will not find a team with only Stars. You have the more tragic teams in which many Question-Marks have been brought together. There are dysfunctional teams where everyone is on the left side of the quadrant. Most teams have some Jerks, Stars, Questions-Marks, and Flops. A manager can ensure balance through proper control of and adherence to core values, open feedback and taking tough decisions when they are needed.

# WATCH OUT: AN ICEBERG!

Negative behaviour can be influenced. You can turn a Jerk or a Question-Mark back into a Star. You should, however, look for the causes of that behaviour, for what lies below the surface. What can you do to monitor the norms and values in the organisation? What makes someone a Saboteur, a Plotter, a Jerk or a Star? Behaviour can indeed be clarified but you must look deeper. The behaviour you see is the tip of the iceberg. Below that there are three more layers that tell you why someone behaves the way they do. The underlying iceberg, which is loosely based on Freud (he was also quite fond of looseness, so this is okay) is a tool that you can use. The only thing we see of someone's personality is their behaviour, the proverbial tip of the iceberg. The behaviour is the ultimate result of the values an individual holds. Based on these values, someone gains beliefs in the course of their life, which in turn determines the attitude that he or she will take in different situations. This attitude again determines the behaviour that someone will exhibit. Are you still following? Yes? Nice. The essence is very simple: get to know the other or yourself. If you want a different kind of behaviour from the other, ask for a different behaviour. Do you want to exhibit other behaviour yourself? Then, which beliefs are you willing to set aside?

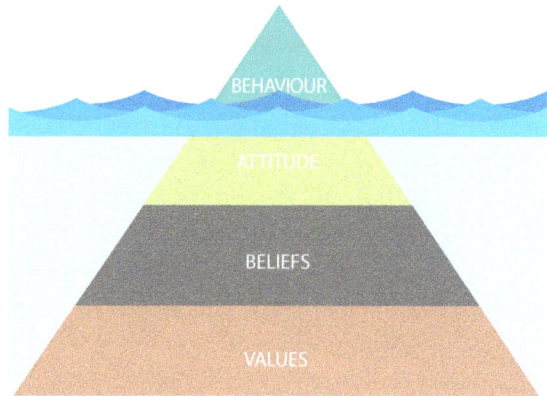

*Figure 7. Personality as an iceberg (Freud)*

## BEFORE IT MELTS

If you believe that you can be a good manager, you probably behave in a way on the work floor that shows this. Your attitude is positive to your own work, your colleagues and your organisation. The confirmation that you show the correct behaviour is shown by the fact that you are on the list of people to be promoted to manager.

If you have the belief that you outperform your colleague to your right, but you get a worse rating for the third year in a row, you can bet your belief is incorrect. The cause of this is set in your values. It could be nurture because at home your parents appreciated perfection. It might be a belief you have gained in the course of your life: I am the best because I always got straight As at school. Or more subconsciously, you may feel superior because you always got picked first with sports. This belief that you are infallible will determine your attitude and behaviour. It may very well be that this belief seriously annoys your manager: you are not open to feedback, do not want to learn from your colleagues, or you are too occupied with your work because it must be done to perfection. Knowing your beliefs can help you change your attitude and behaviour.

Every conviction influences your attitude and, consequently, your behaviour not only in the workplace but at home too. To understand this, consider the belief that has prevented you from stop smoking. Or the belief that makes you go on a diet over and over again. Or the belief that everything should stay the same. Or the belief that there must be something after life.

## FREUDIAN SHAKESPEARIAN

If you want to understand someone's behaviour, it is good to know more about their values and beliefs. Brutus has values that make treason acceptable. Loyalty is either missing or is debatable in his set of values; he believes to be Caesar's peer. The people who want to overthrow Caesar sense this and manipulate Brutus's belief. They are so cunning that Brutus is prepared to betray his boss. His attitude towards Caesar has changed as evidenced by his traitorous behaviour, the dagger's thrust.

Iago's behaviour is more complex. To understand him, you should know more about his background, his education. It is obvious that he is in conflict with the values of both his old and his new environment. The army, as he knows it, changed dramatically after the arrival of Othello. In addition, there is something that convinces him that he is entitled to an important position. That is the reason for him not to accept Othello's authority. His attitude and the traitorous behaviour that follows is a logical consequence. Othello, in turn, has difficulty in understanding the values of his new environment because of his origins. He is hired because of his distinctive attitude to warfare but must also adapt to his environment. Shakespeare lets his characters struggle with conflicting values. Again and again.

## VALUES IN PRACTICE

The values of an organisation are a means of communication between leaders and managers and employees about what really matters in the organisation. What are the reasons for the organisation's existence? Good values match the organisation's strategy and must be taken literally. When it comes to trust: what does the organisation understand that is? When it comes to passion: how does it matter? When it comes to integrity: what is that exactly? Be frank about what is important to the organisation and mean it. If the financial result is the only thing that counts, fine, just say that. Do not hide that goal in other values as appreciation or passion. Remember that honesty and openness are also important values.

The leadership of the organisation has the most important role here. Not only by giving a good example but also by supporting management in complying with these values. Core values give an organisation the possibility to change the workplace - change of direction of the organisation, change in the behaviour of the employees.

## INTEGRITY

Opposite betrayal and deceit is purity of character: integrity. A person of integrity is honest and sincere, trustworthy, says what he does and does what he says. Shakespeare uses integrity to morally elevate one of his characters above the other. These characters have a great deal of authenticity as it is illustrated by the beautiful words coming out of the mouth of a Roman general: "Would you have me false to my nature? Rather say I play the man I am."

## WISE MAN, OLD MAN, STUPID MAN

You have certainly heard: 'Experience is the best teacher' or 'age before beauty'. What's the truth? When it comes to the wisdom or foolishness of King Lear, Shakespeare is rather economical with the truth; he is strange at the best of times. Values in Lear's time are subservience to the king (for God and country) and respect for the elderly. On the basis of that, Lear learned in his long life that he could actually get away with anything. At the end of his life he takes an arrogant and omniscient attitude and drives the people in his environment to their limits. Integrity is not an important value in his court. At least not to him.

*In his eighties, King Lear has it all: a great empire, three beautiful daughters and a powerful life. But his life is coming to an end and the old man decides in all his wisdom (or madness) to leave this world in a grand way. He wants to abdicate the throne and, in a crazy move, he conceives to divide his kingdom among his three daughters. The way he goes about that, however, causes horror at his court: the one who loves him most shall get the biggest piece of the pie - with whipped cream. His two eldest*

133

*daughters don't need any encouragement to praise their father and play the game with pleasure. But his youngest daughter, Cordelia, does not want to flatter him and refuses to participate in this charade. She says she loves him because he is her father and that should suffice him. That is not what Lear expects and he becomes enraged. He bans her, gives his kingdom to the other two daughters, and goes off to live with the oldest one. His loyal advisor Kent tries to save the situation at all costs but that is not easy. Everything that the king has built in his time slowly falls apart. The homecare of his eldest is a complete failure, relationships and loyalty in the royal circles are under pressure, intrigues rule the days, and integrity becomes something unknown to some.*

King Lear is wise enough to gather critics around him. He trusts these people but when he really needs them, he refuses to listen. He raised one of the critics himself, his youngest daughter Cordelia. Her older sisters, on the other hand, are typical Yes-Women and Cheaters. They sweettalk Lear, find everything he does amazing, and overwhelmingly declare their love and affection to him. They are willing to say anything, if that will get them the largest part of his kingdom. Cordelia does not play along. She tells her father that she loves him, but no more or less than that. She believes that this should be enough. In fact, she tells him that he should not need more than that. In her eyes, he lowers himself to a silly old man. Cordelia has integrity, her sisters have not.

## KENT KNOWS CORDELIA

Another person Lear trusts is his loyal advisor Kent. Together with the Fool, he is the only one allowed to hold a mirror in front of Lear so that he can adjust his self-image. His loyalty is put under pressure when Lear wants to divide his kingdom among his three daughters. The king promises all three of them a bonus, but the youngest – the apple of his eye for sure – would get a slightly higher bonus. That is, if she lives up to her father's expectation telling him that she loves him most of all his daughters. Kent knows Cordelia, her candour, her integrity, and smells trouble. She will never do what her father expects her to. In any case, it is unusual to divide your kingdom - and to do that on the basis of love? He advises his sovereign to discard this bad plan but his advice is ignored by the king and he warns him: "Come not between the dragon and his wrath." Kent, who finds the whole situation rather troubling, points out his loyalty to the king, his long-term employment and unconditional commitment. He is just doing his job: to advise the king by acting with integrity. Kent takes his role seriously, however, at that moment, his boss has other expectations from Kent and, especially, from Cordelia.

## TICKLE ME

What the old king expects and hopes does not happen. His two eldest daughters do everything to grab their bonus but, just like Kent had predicted, the youngest refuses to do so. By banning his youngest daughter and Kent from the castle, Lear chooses to reward people who do not question him and agree to everything he says. Integrity appears not to be valuable to the king, so Cordelia and Kent get his finger. Every person enjoys when their ego is caressed and leaders like King Lear have the opportunity to enforce this. After all, they have control over the career of the people working among them. They control their salary, bonus, and promotion opportunities. Everyone is aware of their position and power relations to some degree. Not everyone will be able to go along with their leaders and to put a mirror in front of them at appropriate times. There is always a choice. You can go along with everything or take appropriate action to resolve a difference of insight. Kent also has this choice: to go along or resist. He chooses the first. In disguise, he continues to serve Lear and makes an effort to stick to his advisory role. A lack of integrity in leadership puts pressure on employee's loyalty. When they stay, they adapt, shut up and do what is expected of them. They become Yes-Men and Yes-Women like Lear's daughters. For others, it will start itching and they will start scratching until it hurts so much they have no other choice but to leave the organisation. Some others are like Kent and have the communicative skills to stand up. And every organisation has Cordelias who always stay honest and sincere regardless of the consequences.

## KEEPING UP APPEARANCES

As an 'actor' in your organisation, your manager and

colleagues expect you to adhere to the norms and values. The role you play consists of your professional tasks and the behaviour you show. Just like on stage, credibility is important at work: do people believe in what you do? Unless you are a very good actor (note: without quotation marks), this only works if your attitude and behaviour match the role you play. That is the basis of your identity in the organisation: how you think others look at you and what they expect from you. Perhaps you have experienced that this does not always reflect how your manager or colleague sees you. He can think of your role differently and what you should do in a specific situation. These different expectations can lead to a role-conflict: a situation where your expectation does not match someone else's.

## SCENE 7

(A spacious office in a random office building in a random town. On his first day at work, the HR-advisor is very impressed with his new working environment and his colleagues.)

**VP**: Look! This is the signature of our CEO, young

man. If you notice this on a document, you'd better start running.

**HR-advisor**: Run? What do you mean?

**VP**: Yes! Run for your boss (laughs). Do what he asks you to do. He likes matters to be resolved quickly, very quickly. And you might want to know as well that he doesn't like to answer questions.

**HR-advisor**: That's my role? To run for the boss and do stuff just because his signature is on it?

**VP**: (laughs again, a bit louder now) Exactly right, young man. You still have a lot to learn in this company. Here, you need to get some bonusses paid for him.

(The HR-advisor reads the form the VP handed to him)

**HR-advisor**: Uhm, well, if I read this, sorry, but I do have a question. I've noticed that everyone gets one hundred percent of the maximum bonus but I thought half of the bonus is based on personal performance?

**VP**: (sighs) That is correct, in theory. But you have to read carefully, young man. Didn't you notice what the CEO wrote on the paper? "Any short-coming in personal performance is heavily compensated by our financial results."

**HR-advisor**: Isn't that odd?

**VP**: Yes, that is odd. Very, very, very odd. Please make sure the payments are made today, will you? Thanks.

In scene 7 you are witness to a role conflict. The VP knows how things work in the organisation and acts accordingly. The HR advisor struggles with his norms and values and the expectations he has of his new job. What to do now? Agree or oppose? This scene is about integrity and its perception. Can the HR advisor expect the CEO to set a good example and follow internal guidelines? May the same advisor expect that the VP, if the CEO does not, asks about it? Is he allowed, as an advisor, to criticise this decision?

Integrity is under pressure top down. The CEO misuses his position by failing to comply with the norms and values. The VP, in turn, considers it more important that the work is carried out adequately than monitoring his personal integrity and opposing the CEO. He calls on the HR advisor to be loyal to the organisation and to professionally execute the action. That is not a decent thing to do – to say the least. It puts the HR advisor under pressure to cross the limits of his personal integrity. He will be conflicted between the role he wants to fulfil and what is expected from him.

## FIGHT! FIGHT! FIGHT!

Once there is a conflict, you have several options to deal with it. A conflict, in any case, implies statements of opinion, unless it is okay that the conflict persists. Walking away or being sent off like Cordelia are other possible options, of course. The quadrant below shows the style you prefer when you are in conflict. There is no best or worst way. Nevertheless, it is useful to know and control all styles, so that your conflict does not permanently disturb a relationship.

When you compete, your self-interest is paramount. Lear competes with others in the conflict and this is seen more often with people who have absolute power. He runs into the trap that belongs to this style and by doing so he increases the chance of escalation. It is a good style if hard and fast action is required but the challenge is to keep the troops together.

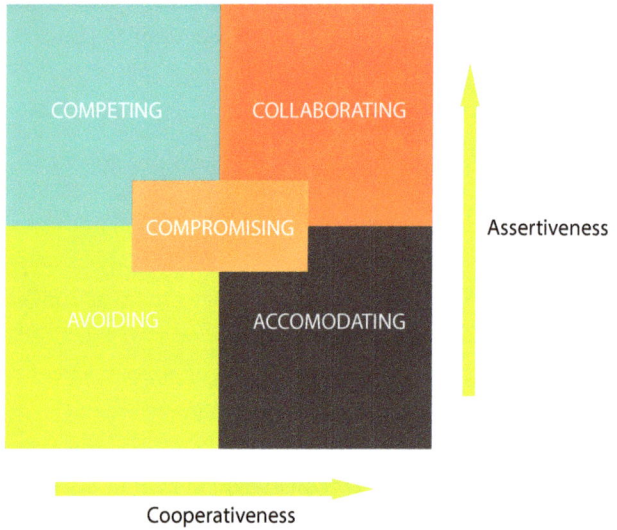

*Figure 8. The conflict model (Thomas & Kilmann)*

Accommodating is the opposite. It is when you fully agree to the interests of the other - a great style if there is a chance that you are wrong or if the subject is more important to the other. It provides credit.

When avoiding, there is no winner and no loser. This style is diplomatic and can be used to bring tension back to an acceptable level. The Fool will continuously look for some sort of conflict, but once it is there, the Fool will avoid it, because it ceases to be important, the point was made a long time before that. So the Fool is already looking for the next conflict.

When exploring, you are looking for solutions that deliver a win-win situation. Kent initially tries to explore and argues why Lear should not divide his kingdom. When he realises that Lear is not going to cave in, he starts to avoid the situation. He takes on a different role and hopes to reach a compromise that can be a temporary solution to a complicated problem. If you are looking for a compromise immediately, there is a chance that you will miss out on a better solution.

Obviously, the Saboteurs, Plotters and other colleagues you have to be mindful of also have a preferred style when it comes to conflicts. You should use the knowledge of these styles to understand them better.

*Figure 9. The favourite conflict styles of deceivers (Renkema)*

## SHORT COURSE ON INTEGRITY

Integrity is by far the most important value in every organisation. Employees who have integrity enable an organisation to monitor other norms and values even if they are under pressure from the outside. Employees with integrity are able to account for their own behaviour and choices. They perform their work well, take account of their responsibilities and the rules. If these are missing or not clear, employees with integrity judge and act in a morally responsible manner and on the basis of generally accepted social and ethical standards.

It is therefore too simple to explain integrity only as the absence of betrayal and deceit. Values such as collegiality, reliability, customer orientation, and effectiveness play a role too. In practice, integrity also means that you can prevent conflict of interests, are able to make your own position and interests clear in potential conflict situations, and that you cannot be bribed. In a conflict, you do not automatically choose the side of the stronger party, but try to take a helicopter view and act on it. You are loyal to the organisation for which you work and you continue to act with integrity even if this entails certain disadvantages, tensions or conflicts for you. Abuse of powers, improper influencing, taking bribes, but also gossip and kissing up to your manager are all examples of acts without integrity.

In order to be able to act with integrity, you must be aware of the values of the organisation and to what extent they align with yours. In your current job, but especially if you change jobs, it's good to look into these values with great attention because it deter-mines the level of success you will have and how much your new employer will make a fit with you.

Your work will continue to appeal to your personal integrity. You will also sometimes feel compelled to comply with the current norms in your organisation. Do you sell yourself short? Sometimes, sometimes not. Consider the advice of one of the characters in Hamlet:

*"This above all: to thine self be true. And it must follow as the night the day, thou canst not then be false to any man."*

## CAN I TRUST ANYONE?

Of course you can. You can trust the vast majority of your colleagues. But if circumstances change, it is wise to look at your current environment with a different lens. For example, after the annual per-formance review circus has been around. Or when the promotions have been awarded. And another moment that would make perfect sense is after a reorganisation. Does anyone whom you trust have a reason to become a Saboteur or Traitor? Do the Yes-Men around you suddenly do something different?

If Julius Caesar had been less blind to the changes in his environment, he could have seen that he was about to be betrayed and by the man who once was his friend. Or was Brutus a Yes-Man who unfolded as a Traitor? If someone feels betrayed like Iago did, it is time to hide. What if Othello took Iago out for a cup of coffee? The thought precedes the emotion and therefore deception is a very powerful fire starter of the most destructive emotions. Iago is a striking example of that. And what is actually the problem of King Lear? Did he want to please everyone? Was he afraid to make a choice? Or did he want to exercise his power one last time? He misuses his power and does not act with integrity in that sense. But is that also the case if there is absolutely nothing in it for yourself?

Shared norms and values within an organisation determine your and your colleague's behaviour. Many organisations have wonderful values that give a soul to the company. What to think of 'Feel free' at Twitter, 'Do more with less' at another company or, especially appealing to some mavericks, 'Create fun and a little weirdness.' If employees recognise them-selves in the values of an organisation then they will soon feel comfortable at home.

What about you, what are your values? Do you detest betrayal and deceit or does it sometimes come in handy? Can you act with integrity in your organisation? Do you know if there are Plotters and Saboteurs in your office and who they are? What kind of company do you work for? Do the values of your organisation speak to you? Do you recognise them? And more importantly, can you feel them?

ACT 4

**SPEA**

OR **BE SILENT?**

*"To be direct and honest is not safe."*

**Othello**

You're a lowlife, a rascal who eats leftover scraps. You're an ignoble, arrogant, shallow, vulgar, pretentious, conceited, filthy third-rate servant who thinks he's something special. You're a cowardly lawyer-loving bastard; a vain, brown-nosing, prissy scoundrel who'd pimp himself out to advance his career; a bag lady." This is how Kent sets the servant of Lear's daughter straight for defying the old King.

On stage, there is not too much time for beating around the bush, so Shakespeare is quite good at providing feedback. Otherwise, the play would take too much time and the audience would not have the patience for that. Consequently, quite a few of his characters show open and direct behaviour in their way of communicating. Sometimes it is a bit rude and sharp around the edges, but in terms of perspicuity it leaves nothing still to be desired. In many organisations, communicating, giving feedback or bringing bad news are major challenges. So what prevails is vague language, avoidance of conflicts, and management terminology. Why do people not just say what they want to say? What makes it so difficult? Open and direct communication are particularly difficult for many people. How do you tell a colleague that he or she has bad breath? Or that you are disappointed in their contribution to the project? Or that you are upset that they are always so negative about their work?

The consensus among philosophers is that this does not happen simply because it is easier. If you say exactly what you mean, you run the risk that it will get messy. People may get angry, sad, confused, or resist your message. Logically, you feel the obligation to clean up that mess - a nasty and time-consuming job that you do not like at all. You trivialise your lack of openness with the argument that you do not want others to feel hurt or pain.

Act Four is about open and fair communication and its battle with lying and keeping silent. What communication style do you recognise in yourself and your colleagues and how do you use this insight? How do you give constructive feedback and what is the importance of sharing information? How do you share bad news? In short: how do you create a safe environment with trust and people talking to each other to prevent betrayal and deceit?

"To be direct and honest is not safe," says the filthy agitator Iago in Othello. Even though Shakespeare likes to steer his audience in the wrong direction, in his plays, honesty is the best policy. Iago, however, is definitely not the living proof of that.

## FIRST AID IN COMMUNICATION

FACI is necessary because communication can hurt. Whether consciously or unconsciously, you may hurt a colleague with your words. Perhaps because you do not know how to communicate with the other or because you do not have the right information or simply because you do not know how to say it. Being authentic helps your conversation partner recognise your honesty. Honesty is your band-aid and authenticity your bandage. Your own values are iodine, compression bandage and tweezers at the same time. What is important to you? How do you want to deal with people? How do you want to be treated yourself?

Communicating is mainly a matter of doing, trying out. Are you uncomfortable saying what you feel or think? Try it out with someone you trust, experience how your message is received and get started. Do you feel like a colleague is in trouble? Ask them about it and help them give a fair answer. Tell them what you see, what you feel and ask if this perception is correct. Nuisances are ongoing on the work floor. How you deal with them is what matters. You might just put your thoughts and feelings out there, but you may come to regret that. You could keep it to yourself to mention it later. You can also let it go because it's really nothing to get upset about. You do not have to be open about everything. The silly dress or the fluffy jacket does not prompt immediately for your comments. Openness is not a means to an end in itself. Remember speech is silver and silence is golden.

## THIS IS HOW YOU COMMUNICATE

To be able to work together effectively, it is important that you communicate openly with each other. The most dangerous pitfall is thinking that the other person thinks just like you. Unfortunately, that is often not the case. And also, the way you appear to be to someone else as well as the behaviour the other is showing, are often quite different from what you would like. Taking a close look at your own behaviour and that of others can help you to avoid this trap. Both verbal and non-verbal behaviour are important because what you do not say but do show, is at least as important as what you say. Your communication style is the sum of all of this.

There are four communication styles. You have your style and the person in front of you has their own style. By knowing your style and recognising the other ones' style, you are able to adapt your way of communicating to the other. This leads to making your communication more effective and working together a lot more fun. Simply because the other person recognises him or herself in you makes them feel comfortable. This is your agility: you are able to take into account the style of your conversation partner and the context of your conversation in your own behaviour.

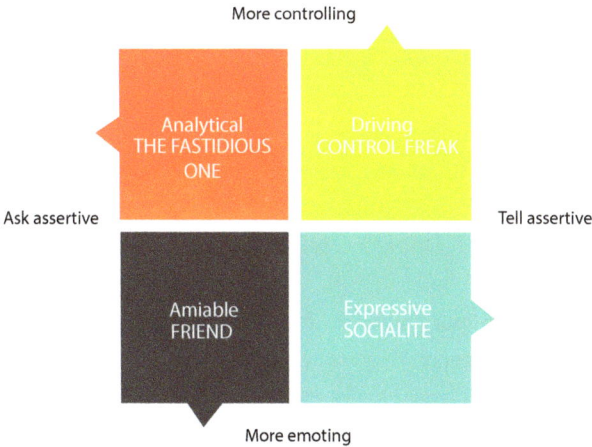

More controlling

| | |
|---|---|
| Analytical<br>THE FASTIDIOUS<br>ONE | Driving<br>CONTROL FREAK |
| Amiable<br>FRIEND | Expressive<br>SOCIALITE |

Ask assertive                    Tell assertive

More emoting

Figure 10. The caps model of personal styles (Merill & Reid)

The model illustrates the way you communicate yourself and with your conversation partner along two axes. The first axis indicates how much space you give in the conversation to the other. How dominant are you and how dominant is the other? The second axis indicates how much of yourself you show in the conversation. This is about introverts versus extraverts.

The four communication styles show what you see and what the other sees of you. The model can help make you more aware of what you are doing and the effect of your behaviour on your interlocutor. After all, you often do things unconsciously, without wondering how it can be done differently.

## THE FASTIDIOUS ONE LOVES DETAILS

The Fastidious One is considerate, examines problems and digs deeply. They will wait diligently for the other to be ready and require many facts before making a decision. The Fastidious One may be seen as boring and formal because of the distance he or she keeps, but is actually the perfect advisor. They solve problems systematically, based on facts and logic. They will always keep a certain distance to protect themselves and often speak softly. They are very precise and can never have too many details. Sudden changes, voice overload and too much attention cause an allergic reaction to them. If you need a lot of information yourself, you will score points with the Fastidious One. If you do not, make sure you are prepared to give as much information as possible to them. Structure your story, make it concrete and substantiate it with facts and arguments. Do that as correctly as possible and be very patient.

## THE FRIEND IS EASY TO GET ALONG WITH

The Friend is cooperative and it is really hard to get into a fight with this kind. Helpful and understanding, they subordinate to the bigger picture. Something they will not show too often is initiative. Friends hate conflicts and are therefore focused on harmonious cooperation. They radiate confidence and express that to the other. Although their style of communication can sometimes be hesitant, Friends are fond of personal interest. Collaborating with a Friend and getting their support can sometimes cost a lot of time.

It is important never to criticise Friends in public as they see this as an unforgivable act. Any form of aggression will also disturb them. Talk to Friends on the work floor as you would talk to real friends in the pub. Ask them about their weekend or family and maintain personal contact. In order to allow Friends to accommodate you, it is important that you are specific about what you want from them.

## THE SOCIALITE LOVES TO HAVE COFFEE

The Socialite is expressive and always nearby if something happens. Socialites are easy going and energetic, and speak at high speed and often in images and associative. They are socially nimble and can sometimes be manipulative. They are competitive, creative and aware of the feelings and emotions of others. The Socialite needs to be appreciated by others. They like to see their warmth and enthusiasm, both word and gesture, reflected in the other. Discipline and 'must do' are not their cup of tea. The Socialite thrives more in a chaotic environment and will not hesitate to attack any opponents to discredit their argument when needed.

If you are not a Socialite yourself, you may have one sitting opposite of you. Try to be more exuberant and more personable in the way you talk. Do not be afraid to reach out to the other and speak longer than usual, make a little chit chat but speak also about more personal matters. Accept that Socialites appear to jump around because of their lack of focus. So do not forget to make clear-cut agreements, because the Socialite will not do that for you.

## THE CONTROL FREAK IS DOMINANT

Control Freaks are directive, active, ambitious, and happy to hold the ropes. They are efficient, focused on results and see risks as a challenge. They sometimes operate as though they have no emotions and are demanding to others. They command authority and leadership, but can become anxious if they lose control. Control Freaks don't like wasting time so greet them quickly and make your point. They will not offer you much space. They often speak monotonously and unless you do not meet the agreed targets, they will not show any emotions. Is your need for control rather low but you do have a Control Freak close to you? Then stick to your subject and focus on the most important facts. Be prepared with your business, be brief, and concise and move on. The Control Freak will appreciate that.

## WHO ARE YOU? WHO? WHO? WHO? WHO?

Having a good conversation is difficult, but if you are able to tailor your communication style to the style of the other, you will find it a lot easier. Initially, it may feel a bit odd, but if you practice it consistently, a whole new world will open up to you.

The communication styles are easy to match to the archetypes from Act One and it is quite all right to place your colleagues in a box. Doing so helps you gain insight into your environment. What's happening around the workplace? What is the reason my colleague shows that behaviour? How can I communicate better with him? It can help you – and your organisation – to progress forward. To clarify this, I mention certain professions that can be stereotypical for the combinations. Of course, these are generalisations so typologies do not apply to everyone in those professions. Two boxes are empty since these are combinations so rare that I have not been able to identify any good examples.

| | SOCIAAL ANIMAL | FASTIDIOUS ONE | FRIEND | CONTROL FREAK |
|---|---|---|---|---|
| CAREER HUNTER | Sales manager | Cardiologist | ? | Management consultant |
| FAN | Royal servant | Payroll administrator | Secretary | Soldier |
| PHILISOPHER | Sociologist | Writer | Middle management | Administrative assistant |
| LOBBYIST | Lobbyist | Psychiatrist | Journalist | Magician |
| ENERGISER | Politician | Accountant | ? | Software architect |
| PARENT | CEO | Head bookkeeper | Family doctor | CEO |

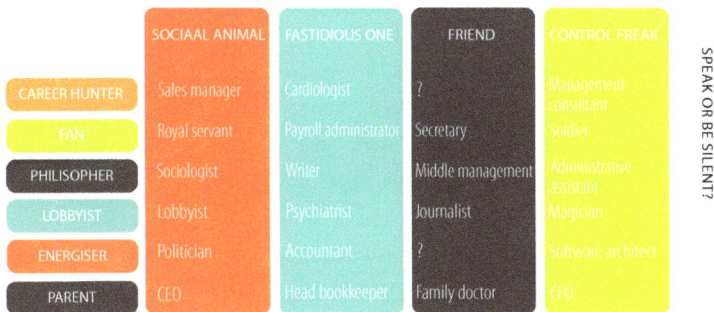

Figure 11. Archetypes and communication styles (Renkema)

## NOTHING WILL COME OF NOTHING

The different communication styles emerge very clearly in Shakespeare's plays, as do the sometimes disastrous effects that result from when dealing with them unconsciously. In King Lear, Lear himself is the Control Freak, his servant Kent is the Friend, and the Fool is the Socialite. His daughter, Cordelia, is, to a certain extent, the Fastidious One. What a lovely bunch, aren't they?

*Cordelia is the youngest of the three daughters of King Lear and the only one who does not sweet-talk her father. She is sincere, honest and thus chooses the hardest way. She could not care less about losing her inheritance. After a lifetime of being worshipped, Lear does not know how to deal with her brutal honesty. He does not understand that the apple of his eye no longer does what he asks of her. Lear wants to continue living in the illusion of his eternal power and does not need her sincerity. He is also oblivious to the openness of both his Fool and his loyal servant Kent. Both have no difficulty expressing themselves whatsoever and have a love-hate relationship with the old man. They would do anything for him but at the same time they do not hesitate to confront him with his shortcomings and sometimes enigmatic decisions. Everybody does that in their own way. Kent knows he is not able to get to the King with his words and has to do the strangest things to show his friendship. Lear tolerates his Fool and occasionally even lends him his ear.*

Cordelia is honest, sincere and has integrity. These are features of the Fastidious One, who also needs a lot of information and details and will always approach things formally. When Lear asks her what she has to say about her love for him, her answer is,

"Nothing, my Lord." Lear almost falls off his throne in astonishment and bites back: "Come on, nothing will get you nothing. Try again." Cordelia replies, "I'm unlucky. I don't have a talent for putting my heart's feelings into words. I love you as a child should love her father, neither more or less." When Lear asks her how she can be so young yet so stubborn she replies by saying she is young and honest. Lear should have known that Cordelia is too principled and too authentic to participate in the folly he has devised. He takes her off guard with this poorly substantiated idea and gives her no time to think about it. Cordelia, the Fastidious One, will dig her graceful heels in.

## AM I ALLOWED TO SAY THAT?

The loyal Lieutenant Kent has the audacity to criticise his boss's decision. Kent speaks of his sense of justice and tries to move him to adjust his conviction: "Kill the doctor who is trying to cure you and pay your decease. If you don't, then as long as I am able to speak I'll keep telling you you've done a bad, bad thing." However, Lear holds himself deaf to his arguments (not so strange at Lear's age) and Kent, increasingly desperate, shows his true character: "What are you doing old man? When powerful kings cave in to flatterers, do you think loyal men will be afraid to speak out against it? When a majestic king starts acting silly, then it's my duty to be blunt. Hold on to your crown and use your better judgment to rethink this rash decision. On my life I swear to you that your youngest daughter doesn't love you least. A loud mouth often points to an empty heart."

Kent does not allow the Control Freak Lear sufficient space to step away from his stupid plan and takes up much more space than the Control Freak feels comfortable with. Because he is surprised by his friend's communication style, Lear can only react with anger. He especially knows him as a friend and loyal servant, and does not understand how Kent dares to talk to him that way. Kent, in turn, should have been more understanding of the emotion of the moment. Lear clearly is delusional and the last thing he needs is someone he holds dear to criticise him. If Kent had spoken to him in private, it might have been more effective, but then the play would have ended after Act 1. You can sometimes bridge a difference of opinion as soon as you know how to communicate properly.

## HERE YOU GO. A MIRROR!

King Lear's Fool is a Socialite. He knows his way with words, is creative and daringly critical. He does not beat around the bush because that is why the King has hired him in the first place. The Fool believes Lear is an idiot, particularly because Lear does not see what an idiot he is. He rejects vanity and authority and adapts his communication style completely to Lear, without compromising the core of the message. That is quite an achievement. He makes use of his authenticity to try and convince Lear of his opinion in order to change his mind. In the next dialogue, you can read how the Fool confronts his sovereign with the disastrous consequences of his decision to divide his kingdom without losing Lear's style of communication out of sight.

## SCENE 8

**Fool**: So, how's it going, uncle? I wish I had two fool's caps and two daughters.
**Lear**: Why, my boy?
**Fool**: If I gave them all I own, I'd have two fool's caps for myself. Here's mine. Ask your daughters

for another one.

**Lear**: Watch out, boy. Remember I can whip you.

**Fool**: I get whipped like a dog for telling the truth, while Lady Bitch gets to stand around the fire and stink the place up with her false words.

**Lear**: A constant pain to me!

**Fool**: I'll recite something for you, guy.

**Lear**: Yes, do that.

**Fool**: Listen up, uncle:

*Have more than you show,*

*Speak less than you know,*

*Lend less than you owe.*

*Ride more than you walk,*

*Don't believe everything you hear,*

*Don't bet everything on one throw of the dice,*

*Leave behind your booze and your whore,*

*And stay indoors,*

*And you'll end up with more*

*Than two tens to a twenty*

**Kent**: That makes no sense, fool. It's nothing.

**Fool**: In that case it's like the words of an unpaid lawyer. You paid me nothing for it. Can't you make any use of nothing, uncle?

**Lear**: Why, no boy: nothing can be made out of

nothing.

**Fool** (to Kent): Please tell him that his income is nothing, now that he's given his lands away. He won't believe a fool.

**Lear**: You're a bitter fool.

**Fool**: Do you know the difference, my boy, between a bitter fool and a sweet one?

**Lear**: No son, tell me.

**Fool**: Bring here

The gentleman who advised you

To give away your land.

You can stand in his place.

The sweet and bitter fool

Will appear right away.

**Lear**: Are you calling me a fool boy?

**Fool**: Well, you've given away all your other rightful titles. The title of fool is the only one left.

## NO CANDOUR? HOW COME?

The Fool knows exactly how to get on the nerves of King Lear. Shakespeare uses candour in his characters to provoke both opponents and audiences. It is his way of practicing politics and advocating his ideas through his plays. The Fool could not care less about Lear's status and reputation. He analyses the situation in which Lear finds himself and says what everyone thinks: Lear has become completely mad to divide his kingdom among his daughters. Politics and madness is a widely used combination, even today. The king seems blind to the truth, but if he shows his vulnerability, the Fool offers him a look in the mirror in a very loving way. Lear is insane for giving up everything and that makes him a fool.

In fact, keeping things to yourself is not a very social thing to do. A lack of openness and feedback in an organisation results in an environment where there is no discussion, no ideas are brought forward and criticism is sugar-coated. There is little that causes more damage to an organisation than a lack of candour. Candour ensures people are involved and engaged. New ideas emerge, people share information and learn from each other keeping everyone involved so no one has an excuse for not participating. In addition, openness is also good for the bank. Imagine how many tedious meetings or unresolved conflicts exist because of a lack of openness.

Candour is refreshing. Everyone has it inside of him,

with no one having more than anyone else. This has everything to do with honesty and authenticity. It depends on your own attitude how you deal with openness and the emotions that come into play. Do you go for harmony and try to avoid differences of opinion or do you go for candour? Unfortunately, the reality is that candour often makes people nervous. It is sometimes easier to cover a message with a layer of pink frosting to make it easier for you. The ability to be open depends on human nature and the beliefs you have. Consequently, it is a big challenge to create an open culture in which everyone feels free and comfortable expressing themselves. An open dialogue can start anywhere. You can start by setting an example of candour by giving compliments to everyone who follows you. Talk about it because an open dialogue can start practically anywhere.

However, an open dialogue cannot happen without you lending your ear to someone else. As we learn to speak well, we do not necessarily learn to listen. In an open dialogue, you should avoid losing yourself in your thoughts thus losing focus on the conversation. Do not try to think about solutions during the conversation and certainly not for the others. Listen, talk and let others speak. Do not lose yourself in the drama that can be the result of a conversation. Do not try to rationalise everything to put it in perspective. Do not overload the other with your questions. Talk, listen and have a dialogue.

## EXTREME CANDOUR

Dutch stand-up comedian and a true master of insults, Hans Teeuwen, once said: "A good insult is to some people the truth they do not want to hear." And that is exactly how Shakespeare uses insults. To him, insult in his plays had a function. It was first and foremost to entertain the public, because there had to be some laughter too. It also says a lot about the characters of both the offender and the one insulted. Can someone tolerate an insult? What is their reaction when insulted? What characters are ignored? Who can only communicate violently? An offense can therefore arise from honesty, but that does not mean it is always appreciated. But an insult does not always have to lead to a conflict, as Cassius explains to Brutus: "This rudeness is a sauce to his good wit, which gives men stomach to digest his words more easily." Shakespeare was

extremely creative when it came to insults and cursing.
So creative that it is the nightmare of every transla-
tor to do it right. In King Lear, Shakespeare draws his
entire registry open when Kent goes berserk: "You're
a lowlife, a rascal who eats leftover scraps. You're an
ignoble, arrogant, shallow, vulgar, pretentious, conceited, filthy third-rate servant who thinks he's something special. You're a cowardly lawyer-loving bastard;
a vain, brown-nosing, prissy scoundrel who'd pimp
himself out to advance his career; a bag lady. You're
nothing but a lowlife, a beggar, a coward, and a pimp,
the son and heir of a mutt bitch. I'll beat you until you
whine and cry if you deny the least bit of this."

## JUST SAY IT!

Shakespeare lets his characters act differently than
they actually are. This creates the much-needed tension in a play. In King Lear, Kent returns to the court
in disguise. In Hamlet, the murdered father appears
unexpectedly as a ghost. In Othello, Iago is a jolly old
chap, but at the same time he deceives everyone. In
many organisations, people too are in disguise or act
differently than they really are. And just like on stage,

it causes tensions: employees who are still a mystery to their employer and colleagues after years of loyal service. What information do you share at work and what not? What do you know about a colleague and what does he know about you? And do you know that of each other? What information does your manager share and what does he keep to himself, hidden from you and your colleagues? Is there something that no one in the team knows?

## OPEN THE WINDOW

The Johari Window is a good instrument for understanding what information is public and what is not. Two ideas are the foundation of the window. The first is that people start trusting each other more when information is shared. The second idea is that with good feedback from others your own arena will grow, your blind spot will be smaller and you will learn about yourself. The window can be used on individual and team level.

The Arena contains information that is known to everyone and can be communicated freely. In an efficient team, it should in any case be about the common goals and the role everyone has. Making the most of this free space is a challenge for every organisation and employees. The larger the Arena, the more effective the mutual communication.

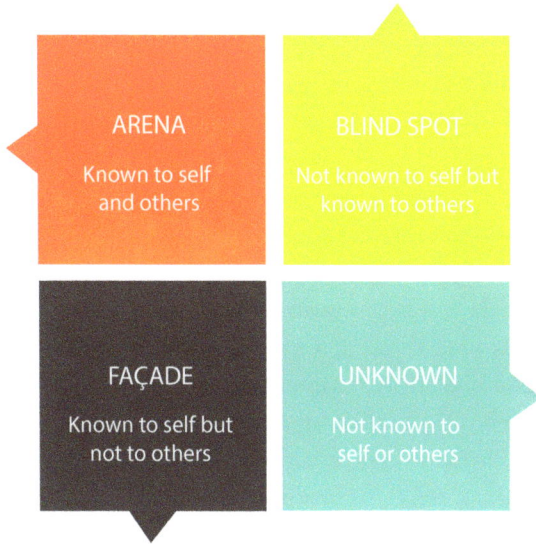

| ARENA | BLIND SPOT |
|---|---|
| Known to self and others | Not known to self but known to others |
| FAÇADE | UNKNOWN |
| Known to self but not to others | Not known to self or others |

Figure 12. The Johari Window (Luft & Ingham)

The Blind Spot in the window is information that others have about you but you do not have about yourself.

It can be something simple, such as a bad breath or a tear in your pantyhose. More importantly, it is about essential matters that affect you, but your colleagues have not shared with you. Dare to ask and dare to share: feedback is valuable and helps you to improve by moving your Blind Spots into the Arena. A common Blind Spot is to cause conflicts and always blame someone else. However, you can also be blind to your own talents that others recognise in you. A person with a big Blind Spot is often unaware of the impact of his or her behaviour and communication on the team.

The information that is only known to yourself is the Façade and is concealed from the others. Sometimes it is used to manipulate colleagues and play power games. More often, things are too personal to share, but do have an effect on your performance. Sometimes it is better to keep certain things to yourself, especially when it comes to confidential information of which you are unsure if the other is able to deal with it and not breach its confidentiality. For example, consider questions about your sexual orientation during a job interview or questions about your private life during in a performance review. You do not blindly have to share everything.

The Unknown area contains the great 'what we do know / what we do not know' -mystery and is therefore very interesting. Reducing the Unknown area by collaborating and investigating will boost employees and teams. This window contains information, feelings, unknown talents and experiences. They can be close to the surface or be hidden in someone's personality, but in such a way that they affect the behaviour. This window refers to skills or aptitude for activities that are paid little attention to, for which there is no opportunity to explore or which are simply not encouraged in an organisation. Discovering this is a big challenge and an adventurous trail that can help the organisation to become more creative and innovative. It depends on who makes the discovery whether this new information goes to the arena, remains hidden or becomes a blind spot. Not everyone is open to new self-awareness or the road that leads to it.

## SCENE 9

(The HR-manager is behind his desk, door is open. Nevertheless, the manager knocks and waits in the door opening. He plucks his vest until he can come in.)

**Manager**: I really wanted to have a word with you about a matter that is extremely confidential. Consequently, you will have to allow me to close the door.

**HR-manager**: Please do Edward.

**Manager**: I am concerned that Ella might leave us.

**HR-manager**: What do you mean?

**Manager**: Well, I believe she is about to leave the organisation. At least, that is what I suspect.

**HR-manager**: Is there some ground for that suspicion Edward?

**Manager**: It is a feeling.

**HR-manager**: Okay, a feeling, always tricky. You haven't asked her, have you?

**Manager**: Asked her what?

**HR-manager**: If she is planning to resign.

**Manager**: If she is planning to resign?

**HR-manager**: Yes. That. Have you asked? That's what you'd like to know right?

**Manager**: Heavens no, of course not. That is not something you just simply ask someone? Suppose she say yes?

**HR-manager**: At least you have your answer.

In scene 9 everything comes together. The HR manager and manager both are unaware of the employee's intention. For both, this is an Unknown area, but not for the employee. If Ella indeed wants to leave the organisation, it is part of her Façade. If this is not the case, then the fact that her manager is suspicious of her leaving is a Blind Spot. Just as the manager has a Blind Spot when it comes to his style of leadership. The HR Manager gives him a subtle hint, you can hardly call it feedback. However, it seems to have landed and the manager can take steps to bring the information to the Arena. He has to ask a difficult and dangerous question: 'Are you considering leaving the organisation, Ella?' Each answer makes the Arena larger, but will also require an action from him. Another situation that proves the Philosophers are right. It is easier, and safer, for the manager to sit on his hands and do nothing. He has done that for a while, but there comes a time when he has to step out of his comfort zone.

## HERE YOU GO, SOME FEEDBACK

There could be many reasons for not giving your colleague feedback: you are too busy, it is too hard or you are quite sure the other person knows it already. There are also plenty of reasons not to hear or listen to the feedback of others: you think the other person does not understand you, you know yourself just fine, or the ultimate knockdown argument 'I have been working here for a very long time'. Giving and receiving feedback is important because that is the only way to make the Blind Spot and the Façade smaller and the Arena larger. A large Arena indicates that everyone in the team has the information needed to communicate and perform well. For you personally, it means that you have more than enough information to function properly. If you have a small Façade, you give your manager and colleagues sufficient information to work well with you. By giving feedback to the other and exposing yourself, you can increase trust in each other. At Google, teams organise feedback meetings themselves. Colleagues encourage each other to share their professional fears so that they can be discussed. On top of making the Façade smaller, the real bonus is that they also discover that many fears prove to be completely unfounded.

The give and take of the feedback process also brings information from the Unknown area to the Arena. You have an 'aha experience' if you can connect the dots. Think of the withdrawn and sad looking colleague who finally talks about their sick child. Think of the customer who drives a hard bargain until a colleague makes you aware of a new product that the customer is actually waiting for. Think of your manager who knows how to change his or her style after receiving feedback from you and your colleagues.

Giving and receiving feedback is often experienced as threatening. It takes a lot of time and effort to do it well. You need to develop sensitivity and the ability to empathise with the other. Look at yourself critically to make your feedback valuable. If you give feedback, be specific about what you see and do not leave it to the other person to interpret what you see. You will avoid unnecessary emotions. If a colleague is unusually silent during a meeting, you do not say 'you were very absent during the meeting' but rather, 'I noticed that you only spoke twice in a two-hour meeting.' Good feedback also includes a sense of reflection on your part, such as: 'I felt alone' and an action point, such as: 'Could you please participate more actively next time?'

If you get feedback yourself, indicate what you are going to do with the feedback and do not act defensively. It is usually not a personal attack. Ask for clarification if you do not understand, show appreciation and treat the person giving you feedback with respect. This keeps the relationship open and improves how you work together.

Strangely enough, giving negative feedback is often perceived to be easier than giving positive feedback. Or we simply forget giving feedback because we find it self-evident that someone did something good. Feedback is best if there is a good balance between positive and negative. Do not forget to give compliments, plenty of them in fact, so you do not have to reach for the first-aid kit.

## THE GLASS IN THE WINDOW

The size of the various Johari Windows will vary from person to person. Some people have a large Façade while others embrace the Arena. There are colleagues with countless Blind Spots and others who have no problem with receiving feedback whatsoever. In any case, these windows will influence the team and your performance.

## CLEAN WINDOWS

A large Arena is a sign of great trust in your colleagues as well as good, consistent and structured forms of feedback. You are an open book to most of your colleagues and that trust pays off because they also share more with you. You do not necessarily have to have a large Arena with everyone. Colleagues who are not close to you may perceive your candour inappropriate or even threatening because of the limited relationship they have with you. In the team, there is candour and mutual understanding by sharing personal information. Everyone freely gives and receives feedback. The more open you are to others, the fewer (mind)games are played.

183

## KNOCKING ON A LOZENGE

If your Façade and Arena are more or less the same size, you are likely to ask a lot of questions of others but you do not return the favour by sharing an equal amount of information or feedback. You want to know the position of others before committing yourself to the one or the other. You are an interviewer. This makes it difficult for your colleagues to determine where you stand. It is quite possible you will end up in a situation where they are fed up with your attitude and that they will not share any information with you anymore because of a lack of trust. You cannot blame them, can you? If you ask how it is going with the other or inquire about their opinion without revealing something about yourself, you have got this coming.

## A BRICK THROUGH THE WINDOW

If you recognise this, you could just be the well-known bull in the china shop. Your Blind Spot is as big as your Façade. You tell your colleagues exactly what you think of them, but could not care less about what others think of you. You are able to lash out verbally to your colleagues or to criticise the team as a whole. For one reason or the other you are either insensitive to the feedback of the people around you or you just do not care. Either way, listening is not your strongest point and consequently your colleagues will turn away from you. They stop talking to you. The result: you actually have no idea how others look at you or what impact you have. Your behaviour is ineffective and you do not know how to correct that.

## MIRRORGLASS

| | |
|---|---|
| ARENA | BLIND SPOT |
| FAÇADE | UNKNOWN |

A large Unknown area is especially seen in younger people or colleagues with less experience in their field of expertise or in the organisation. Your self-consciousness is limited and your team knows even less about you. You can also be the silent force nobody ever asks or who never asks for anything. Your colleagues have trouble understanding you and your position. You are a mystery and have erected a large wall around you. If a colleague dares to ask you why you are not that vocal, you will most likely reply with the excuse that you learn more by listening. The wall stops people but also stops you. It will cost you quite a lot of energy to keep this up. Good luck, stranger!

## THE VENETIAN WINDOW-PANE

Façades and Blind Spots are important tools for Shake-speare. He actively used them in the first acts of his pie-ces for a fantastic dramatic effect. To the public, who are literally and figuratively in the arena, he reveals in due course of the play step by step who manipulated, lied, or was actually open. In the last act, all informa-tion is on stage and the play itself reaches its climax.
The characters in Othello have many Blind Spots and some enormous Façades. Except Emilia, who has no difficulties in sharing her most bold and intimate thoughts.

*Do not underestimate the force of an angry woman - a very angry woman. Emilia works for Othello, you know, the extremely jealous general in the previous Act. She has a lot of faces - some of them are quite nice, others not so. She says what she thinks and men should really know they cannot walk over her. Most of all she is a loyal friend to Desdemona. But she is married to Iago, you know, that fascist from the previous Act. Des and Em had daily tea parties where the one, Des, spoke highly of her love for her husband and the other, Em, was actually sick and tired of her marriage with that huge twerp. The irony wants Em's husband to be the agitator who convinces Othello that Desdemona is cheating on him, but they find out way too late.*

Desdemona is quite troubled by the fact that her husband Othello thinks she is cheating because she could not imagine any woman being capable of that. Emilia has her own thoughts about it and gives her some feedback: "But I do think that it is the husband's fault if we wives cheat on them. For instance, our husbands may stop sleeping with us, and give it out to another woman instead. Or they may get insanely jealous, and keep us from going anywhere. Or let's say they hit us, or cut back on the money they give us out of spite. Makes us vindictive [...] Then let them treat us well. Or let them figure out that the bad things we do are just what we learned from them."

As true friends, Des and Em share everything with each other. Emilia does not beat around the bush and tells what she sees and feels. Even if it is upfront and feminist, which is quite unusual behaviour for a woman in the seventeenth century. There is a big Arena, their

Façades are small and the Blind Spots are very limited, however painful that may be at times. They both have the same Blind Spot: the gossip that Iago spreads over Othello and Desdemona. Emilia's openness is to be praised and she helps her friend to see the events in perspective.

How different is that with her husband, Iago, who is lying and scheming to ruin general Othello. He has no honesty; his Façade is enormous and the only interest he has is to keeping Othello's Blind Spot as large as possible. Iago is a smart cheater. He hints Othello that he knows things that Othello himself does not know. The general accuses Iago of lack of openness: "You are not being a good friend, Iago, if you even think your friend has been wronged and you do not tell him about it."

This is the essence of feedback. Unfortunately, what Iago whispers in his ear about the affair between Cassio and Desdemona are pure lies: "What if I had said I saw him do something to hurt you? Or heard him say something about it. You know there are jerks out there who have to brag about bedding some woman …. ." Othello goes into a frenzy about such suggestion and that makes Iago happy: "Keep working poison! This is the way to trick gullible fools. Many good and innocent women are punished for reasons like this."

## SORRY, I NEED TO TELL YOU SOMETHING

In the seventeenth century, a messenger is a profession. Conveying a message, particularly if it involves bad news, is not without risk. Don't shoot the messenger should be taken literally. Nowadays, you will still hear these words of warning whenever there is news about lay-offs, a reorganisation or malperformance. Being the bearer of bad news is a frightening thought for many and egos shrink to the size of a sultana looking at the anxious face at the other side of the table. Stuttering, sweating and escapism are the symptoms, bad news the cause.

## SCENE 10

(A cafeteria in a random office building in a random city. Two colleagues, both of them in sales, are eating a club sandwich.)
**One colleague**: I finally met the CEO yesterday.
**The other colleague**: Junior or senior?

**One colleague**: Senior.

**The other colleague**: There's no stopping that guy, is there? Pretty amazing to be in the office every single day when you are seventy-eight. Built it with his own two hands; makes it hard to retire.

**One colleague**: He stopped me in the hallway and pulled me into his office.

**The other colleague**: Oh really? How so?

**One colleague**: Well, I am about to tell you. He picked up a proposal from his desk and asked if it was mine.

**The other colleague**: And?

**One colleague**: It was mine. Guess what happened next?

**The other colleague**: Well?

**One colleague**: He throws that same proposal on the carpet and starts jumping up and down on it, yelling at me: 'This is bad, bad, bad.'

**The other colleague**: You've always been a bad boy.

(Both of them laugh and continue eating.)

In any case, this bad message is brought into the open

directly. Perhaps not too constructive but scene 10 could just as easily have ended in a dismissal or tough performance review. This is the hidden message in the wrath of the director. As founder of the company, he feels a great responsibility and takes the trouble to bring bad news himself.

Everyone is the bearer of bad news from time to time, not just managers or directors. If you want to be open, there is no getting away from it. Just think of Iago: "You are not being a good friend, Iago, if you even think your friend has been wronged and you do not tell him about it." Awareness of the different Johari Windows can help. Is a bad performance review still bad if someone has had good and concrete feedback about his work all year long, or is it a logical consequence? If you are applying for a new job and your manager is aware of this, is your resignation then bad news or a logical consequence? Openness, diminishing Façades and Blind Spots can soften bad news. That makes it a bit easier.

In theory, most people know how to give bad news, but putting it into practice requires a lot more resilience. Practice makes perfect and you must avoid the following three pitfalls. The first is that you want to go too fast. It is definitely good to bring the message right away, but that does not mean that the conversation immediately ends. So, do not check your phone for mail immediately after but help your colleague to process the news. The second pitfall is not being straightforward and honest. You are trying to let the other hang himself. You manipulate the situation by asking questions like 'do you think our project is going well?' or 'how often have we been talking about your inability to change?' With every question you ask, you get closer to the scaffold and before you know it you dangle yourself because you have given away control over the conversation. The last pitfall is being too slow. You have a difficult conversation but you first go out and get some coffee. Or suddenly you are curious about how your colleague's aunt's cousin is doing. With each sentence you utter that does not make sense, getting the message across becomes a lot more difficult.

## THE ELIZABETHEAN CURVE

Bad news always evokes emotions, no matter how you do it. By avoiding the pitfalls, it is possible to limit the impact on the person receiving it and the respective (work) environment. That is the baseline you want to achieve if you have to continue to work together and makes life easier for both of you. But also when you have to tell someone they are fired, you just want to be able to meet the other person on the street without having to duck into an alley. The following curve is a good representation of the stages someone goes through when experiencing a negative change. You may have experienced this yourself when you had to give bad news to a friend or colleague. Or perhaps you have witnessed it with the colleague who just had a bad review.

The first response to bad news is denial or despair, depending on whether or not someone saw the message coming. Either way, the next reaction is anger. That can be immediate or delayed, but do not be mistaken, anger will come. Everyone responds differently and one person may need longer to go through the different stages than the other. Do not make the mistake of thinking that 'not so bad' news results in less fierce emotions. One can be furious if they cannot follow a training while another may be relieved if there finally is clarity about their redundancy. If a colleague gets bad news, it depends on their Façade whether they share it with you or not. A large arena has great advantages even with bad news.

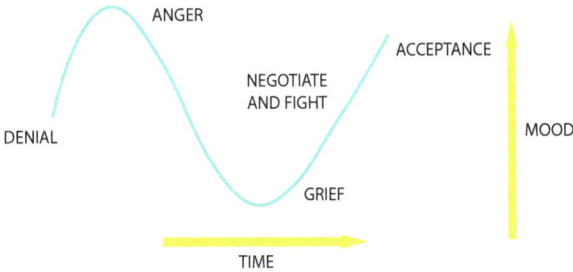

Figure 13. The change curve (Kübler-Ross)

If you have to bring bad news yourself, the following may help to soothe the pain. Listen, but do not comfort the other, because it should not be mixed with bad news. Make sure you explain the reasons for the bad news briefly and concisely. Always play the ball, not the individual, and listen to what the other person has to say. Know that the other is busy absorbing the bad news and consequently does not want to understand anything at that point of time. Therefore, do not count on comprehension and always use the same words if you have to explain the rationale again. Finally, the biggest gift you can give someone is a solution. In concrete terms, do what is arranged without expiring details. When the time has come to say goodbye to someone, do it well. There should be no surprises or no humiliation just straight forward professional delivery of the message.

## THE HAMLET CURVE

In King Lear one after another gets bad news: Lear that his daughter does not want to declare him her love; Cordelia, that her father wants to ban her; and Kent that he has been fired. They all deal with it in a different way. Lear continues to be in denial and remains angry. Only later, when he feels his end is near, sorrow and acceptance sink in. Cordelia and Kent are moving fast through the stages because they want to keep working on a good understanding with their father and sovereign, respectively.

In Othello, the general cannot believe that his wife is cheating on him and that thought makes him sad, very sad. Once he is convinced that she shares the sheets

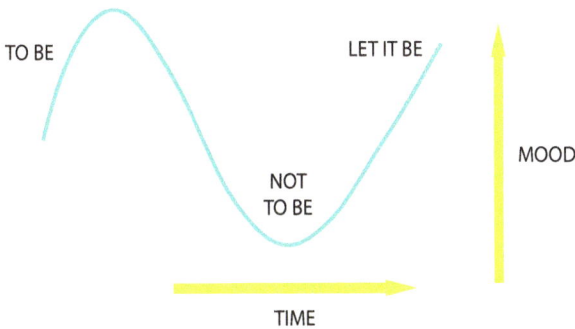

Figure 14. Hamlet curve (William & Wiemer)

with another, he is outraged. He kills her (bad news for Desdemona), burst into tears, and accepts his destiny. Actually, Shakespeare has been the first to define these different stages in Hamlet.

## HONESTY: WHAT A POOR DEVIL

How much candour can an organisation tolerate? How open should you be? What is the best way to communicate in a professional environment? Shakespeare makes his characters speak briefly and concisely, because on stage there is no time for a tedious meeting that takes hours to decide on a conflict. For those who read the plays accurately, there is a lot to learn and discover about communication, may it be: between man and woman; between manager and employee; or between friends.

In any case, his plays teach you that leaders should set a good example and what can happen when they do not. Henry from Act One takes the lead by being open and keeping no information away from his army. His commanders and soldiers reward him with an amazing victory. King Lear shows that lack of communication about the plans you have with your kingdom can lead to negative behaviour and the disintegration of your empire. People follow the behaviour they see. Leaders are thus able, consciously or unconsciously, to create forms of communication and behaviour that can influence an organisation positively but also negatively.

A safe environment in which people trust one another and are free to talk to each other starts with the leaders who set the tone with their style of communicating. It is important to know what style you are using and which one your colleague use. Giving feedback should be as normal as getting a coffee from the vending machine, having the burgers in the cafeteria, and Christmas in December. Give feedback and share compliments. Work on your Blind Spots and enlarge your team's Arena. If your Façade resembles a suit of armour, dare to expose yourself. Do not be afraid of bad news whether you are giving or receiving it. What is the worst thing that could happen to you?

What about you? Who are you? The Fastidious One or the Control Freak? Do you dare to tell the person in front of you what you think of them? Are you comfortable asking them how they feel about you? Do you know how your way of communicating comes across to others? What is it getting you and what it is costing you? How big is your Façade? How about your Blind Spot? Do you like to speak or is silence golden? Is it safe to be honest in your organisation?

ACT 5

**SPOTLIGHT**

OR **BLACKOUT?**

*"If Chance will have me King, Chance may crown me, without my stir."*

**Macbeth**

Royal blood is the only selection criterion for succession to the throne. Sometimes it works out, sometimes it does not and, in the seventieth century, Shakespeare wrote about both cases.

For the famous Henry V, whom we met in the First Act, things worked out quite well. He exceeds his father's expectations as well as those of his people. He is quite the opposite of his equally famous predecessor Richard III, who creates a bloody mess when he takes possession of the crown. On the other hand, Shakespeare would have written a beautiful play about when things don't go quite as well, starring the most famous and colossal blunder in recent history, Edward VIII. Here is one who has no desire to wear the crown and when he falls in love with a divorced and American born woman, his royal fate is quickly sealed. He found himself forced to abdicate – by the way, not a first in English history. This is the incident that unexpectedly freed the way for a second Elizabeth on the English throne a few decades later. And she has managed to keep that crown on her head for longer than her illustrious predecessor and namesake. Sometimes a good succession plan is a coincidence.

Promotion and succession are in line, but a promotion does not necessarily mean that you succeed someone. Promotion can be seen all across an organisation as part of an employee's career path. Succession planning is usually about the top dogs and consequently has a greater strategic importance and more impact on the organisation. Many organisations acknowledge that a good and transparent promotion and succession planning policy is crucial to success. At IKEA, for example, you will only be eligible for a promotion if you have a trained successor. At General Electric, every manager knows that when he resigns, he will find his successor behind his desk the next morning, because no one is bigger than the organisation. However, there are at least as many companies struggling to fill key positions or to have a solid promotion process.

Succession planning, promotion and demotion are the serious topics in this Act. What can you do to qualify for promotion? How do you prevent jealousy, colleagues who leave when they are not promoted and making the wrong choices? What makes it so difficult for employees to take a step back? How does an organisation ensure continuity in leadership? Act Five is partly drama - the drama of the unfortunate employee who does not get the promotion or needs to take a step back; the drama of the boardroom battle when it comes to succession. Where drama is one side of the medal, appreciation is the other side. How do you celebrate a promotion and with whom? How do you take your first steps as a leader of an organisation and when is it time to close the door behind you?

# WHAT AN UNGRATEFUL DOG!

Most organisations set criteria for a promotion; it is not automatic. You must not be a jerk. You must meet the standards and values of the organisation and your performance must be excellent. It is not enough that you have distinguished yourself from the other colleagues and you have been around long enough to move on. You are also dependent on how others perceive you and factors that you cannot influence, such as a vacancy or changes in the leadership of an organisation. If you get a promotion, do not expect the entire organisation to be cheering for you. Your position is not yet secure: you have to prove yourself and sometimes even fight with jealous colleagues like an Iago.

*As a dark-skinned general, Othello is used to moving around in a rather Caucasian environment. The people in his sphere find it difficult to get to know him, but his track record and unconventional approach to warfare give him a lot of credit. As soon as he promotes Cassio to be his adjutant on which his colleague Iago counted, all hell breaks loose. In the eyes of Iago, Cassio was nothing*

205

*more than a nerd "that never set a squadron in the field, nor the division of a battle knows more than a spinster, unless the bookish theoric wherein the toged consults can propose as masterly as he is. Mere prattle without practice is all his leadership." To scrutinise both Othello and Cassio, Iago spreads the false gossip that Cassio has an affair with Desdemona, Othello's wife and the love of his life. The constant manipulation of Iago transforms Othello from a calm, wise, and powerful man into a jealous and bitter creature. Below the surface, Othello is quite insecure. His working environment and culture are new to him and his wife, twenty years younger, is from a very distinguished Venetian family. Iago is very conscious of Othello's weak-points and makes optimal use of his knowledge: "The moor is of free and open nature, that thinks men honest that but seem to be so. And will as tenderly be led by th' nose as asses are." Othello eventually erupts in anger. Desdemona denies the rumours passionately, but Othello ends up killing her regardless. When the deception of Iago finally comes to light, Othello takes the life of Iago and his own as the ultimate consequence.*

Othello believes Iago understands why Cassio

received the promotion. This assumption is a fatal assessment error, as we come to know later. Othello prefers Cassio because as a mathematician he has competencies that make a better fit with the requirements of new war fare. Canons are becoming more important and adjusting these canons is a precise and important task. Iago claims to be entitled to the position due to his tenure and his results on old battlefields. For many years he has been dedicated to serving his city and building a good reputation. The new requirements set by Othello for a promotion are a Blind Spot for Iago. Othello has failed to create an open culture in which everyone feels safe to talk to each other. Even for an army, that is unwise. Iago now has a good feeding ground for his intrigues. Should Othello have taken the time to sit down with Iago and explain his reasons, he would have been able to save a lot of lives. But for Shakespeare, that reasonableness would not have created the beautiful drama that is now on paper. Othello is about the dark sides of ambition and shows that without any norms and values any ambition will fall in action and any promotion will fail.

## THIS IS MY SPOT!

A career moves back and forth. Moving up the ladder is sometimes followed by steps aside or steps back to continue your way up. Getting promoted is partly under your own control. Sometimes it is a matter of luck because you happen to be in the right place at the right time. But luck can also be enforced. You can enhance your job and look for extraordinary activities and bold actions to highlight yourself. Surprise your manager and help your colleagues to do an even better job. Changing your job in such a way to exceed the organisation's expectations is the best way to get ahead.

What should you do if you get promoted? What if you have been drinking a beer (and perhaps one beer too many) every Friday with your colleagues talking freely about your organisation and complaining a bit as well? Can you still do that? What is the impact of changing relationships? The fact that you get a promotion will evoke different responses in your environment. In any case, it is your chance to showcase your leadership and increase your communication skills by responding to and dealing with the different responses and emotions.

There are four groups to look for when it comes to reactions on your promotion.

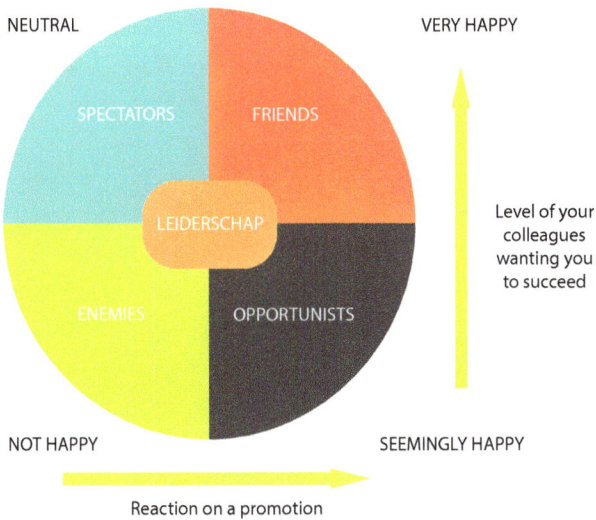

Figure 15. After 'reactions on a promotion' (Welch)

Friends will not begrudge your success and will want you to succeed. Othello is happy for Cassio, not in

MANAGEN OF NIET, DAT IS DE VRAAG

the least because he really needs him for the next battles. The Spectators are indifferent and often more distant from you. The Opportunists suddenly join your table for lunch because they think there is something in it for them too - or they may want to trick you. Iago does exactly that to Cassio because he wants to see him fail. Your Enemies will be known to you straight away. They will ignore you and do everything in their power to undermine your work and your authority. And the motto of the Opportunists (with Iago leading the pack) is, of course, the enemy of my enemy is my friend.

## THIS IS NOT MY SPOT...

Promoting the wrong person can have dramatic consequences. The same applies when you hire externally too. In some organisations, you will automatically get a promotion if you stick around long enough. In other organisations, you get a new position if you are threatening to leave and sometimes the manager has a Blind Spot when it comes to the employee who wants to move up.

# SCENE 11

**Director**: I intend to name Lucas manager of the department.

**HR-manager**: What makes him such a good candidate for the role?

**Director**: Gee, that's a difficult question.

**HR-manager**: What does that say about Lucas?

**Director** (ignoring the remark): Lucas has told me he will leave us if he does not get this promotion.

**HR-manager**: Right…

**Director**: And we really can't afford to lose him.

**HR-manager**: Sounds like blackmail. Does that qualify him as a manager?

**Director**: Come on, don't do that.

**HR-manager**: Lucas is an excellent professional and I do understand you would dread to lose him. But you know just as well as I do he would make a lousy manager.

**Director**: Either way, he is going to get the job.

**HR-manager**: How many employees will leave you think, if he becomes their manager?

**Director**: I don't know. The only thing I know for sure is that he would leave and that is more than enough for me.

The mere fact that someone works well in a certain position does not automatically mean that he will excel in another. This is true for Lucas, who thinks everyone can manage, but also, for example, for the football coach who wants to become a technical director or the pastry chef aspiring to be the chef.

In the months leading to Lucas' departure, nearly a quarter of his team leaves as did Lucas himself ultimately as well. Managing was not quite what he expected. The director did not give Lucas this job with the same scrutiny and judgment he would have taken with an external candidate. Instead of assessing Lucas objectively on his abilities, he more or less gave him the job under coercion, with all its consequences.

The director, like Lucas, sees leadership as the holy grail at work. You only matter if you are on top of the rake and have people reporting to you. It gives a certain status and is a logical step in the careers of many people, without looking into the mirror first. However, there is no position in which you can fail so conspicuously. Returning to his old job is not an option for Lucas, because both he and the director would implicitly be admitting they made an assessment error. Lucas continues to dodge until he decides to leave the organisation.

A long and happy tenure is not always a guarantee of success. Being successful in a solo role does not offer that guarantee either. Someone who is effective in one role is not automatically successful in another role. In a hierarchical organisation like in scene 11 you see that employees are eligible for promotion as long as they perform well. This process continues until someone reaches a position in which he does not meet expectations. That is the Peter Principle. The added value for the organisation decreases and in Lucas' case it even costs money. Lucas' meeting with Peter was not very pleasant.

## ALL RIGHT, I AM LEAVING!

Awarding promotions is all about making choices. Several people may have the skills needed for the open position. The person who did not get promoted can decide to stay or leave.

Some stay because they are agile and always see new opportunities. Some stay to do what Iago did and continue to pursue a promotion at the expense of everything. If you do this and are like Iago, this will ultimately be at your own expense. If you do your utmost to make your own light shine the brightest, you are going to demoralise the people around you by making them feel small. You will do anything to camouflage your own mistakes or - worse - to blame someone else. The Career Hunter in you emerges and this can be the fastest way to sabotage your own career. It might be better just to leave.

Some people leave because they feel they have worked to their maximum but it is always someone else who gets all the credit. For others it is a confirmation that they do not connect well with their manager and that there is no future. It is important to eliminate the disappointment of employees by giving them new aspirations or offering new opportunities for development. Otherwise, they will also be leaving.

The moment will come when it is time to look for other opportunities around – for example, when you did not get the promotion you worked so hard for, or when the right job, that will improve your position, never materialises. Making steps forward sometimes means saying goodbye and accepting that your investment in the organisation will not yield what you expected. Or, to put it in the words of Shakespeare: "If you can't change something, don't cry about it. When you lament something bad that's already happened, you're setting yourself up for more bad news. A robbery victim who can smile about his losses is superior to the thief who robbed him, but if he cries he's just wasting time."

## A STEP BACK

Taking a step back was not in fashion in the seventeenth century. At least, not voluntarily. You remain king until you die. Queen too for that matter - in the United Kingdom this is still common practice. In the Church, taking a step back is not a good sign, and in the army, demotion is a consequence of failure, as Cassio shamefully discovered.

*Cassio is rather pleased with his promotion but his colleague Iago was really upset: Cassio gets the promotion that Iago feels he is entitled to. He literally fights for the job and is angry when he doesn't get it. Really, really angry. In order to successfully take revenge on Othello,*

*Iago knows it is important to smear the reputation of Cassio first. In a cunning way, Iago leads Cassio to believe that he is really happy for him and invites him over to have a glass of wine, knowing Cassio cannot hold his liquor: "If I can fasten but one cup upon him, with that what he hath drunk tonight already, he'll be as full of quarrel and offense as my young mistress' dog." And that is what happens. Cassio gets drunk, finds himself involved in a fight and right when Othello suddenly appears, Cassio punches someone in the face. Iago takes full advantage of the situation and exaggerates the whole incident leaving the general no other choice than to take away Cassio's stripes.*

Degrading an officer is a classic form of demotion as a sanction: someone has stepped out of line and discredited the organisation. Demotion often occurs after a reorganisation or due to malperformance. With a negative connotation like this, it is no wonder demotion is still taboo. It should not be. If you set other priorities in your life, get sick or just older, it's logical that your competencies change or your productivity is reduced. Imagine that David Beckham would still play for Manchester United or John

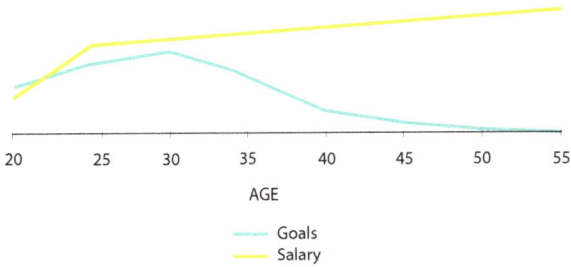

Figure 16. David & John Curve (Renkema)

Barnes for Liverpool FC for the same salary as they earned in their glory days – adjusted for inflation of course. Everybody would find that silly. Somehow, for most other professions, this is a lot more sensitive. A steady line going up in regard to salary is almost taken for granted and considered a right that has been earned over the years even if the added value for the organisation does not show the same upward line.

## EQUILIBRIUM

Managers and colleagues see their younger colleagues dismayed because they do the same work for less money. They see co-workers muddling through in a position that does not fit them anymore, resulting in an inevitable burn-out. Older people may stick around simply because they cannot compete with others in terms of salary and capacity and have no other choice. If you understand the Peter Principle, you will recognise why some colleagues in the workplace are dissatisfied or why a department is functioning poorly. They are in the position where they have to be – according to the principle - only to come to the conclusion that colleagues are difficult, the organisation does not cooperate and the job is too much of a burden. These colleagues eventually disappear in the anonymity of the organisation or depart. They have reached the level of their incompetence. If they stay in the organisation, they are at risk of becoming organisational dead weight. So, if taking a step up is not a viable option anymore - why not take a step back? Our society is so focused on growth and development that this option is not realistic.

It is nonsense to assume that everyone continues to grow and continues to learn and develop throughout his career. Not everyone's productivity will keep track of and stay in line with the progression of salary throughout their career. Many people value their accrued status and salary and have difficulty acknowledging that their skills have not kept up. A voluntary step back is therefore unquestionable for many people and demotion is one of the last taboos in the workplace. And that is too bad because a parity step - another word for demotion - can be good for both the employee and the organisation. It should be absolutely normal to take a step back for whatever reason at a certain point in your life (you have set other priorities like having a child or because you want to reach your retirement in a healthy way or if you want a new balance in your life). With a parity step, you bring your duties, responsibilities and salary in line with your current capacities and private life. You experience less stress, more flexible ways to accomplish your tasks and better balance work-personal life, in exchange for a cut back in salary.

## WELL DONE

Quite rightfully so, employees are taking more and more the route towards a parity step. They expect a form of entitlement from their employer that allows them to balance between what they can deliver and what the employer expects of them throughout their career. This can be achieved by adjusting working hours, proper supervision by the manager, retraining and adaptation of job requirements - just to name a few. Employer and employee both have a responsibility for the parity step: the employee by having a close look in the mirror and the employer by respectfully helping and guiding the employee to a new position. Ultimately, that can only make all parties involved happy.

But how different is that for Cassio? His drunken demeanour leads to a personal and professional disgrace and he is furious about himself: "It hath pleased the devil drunkenness to give place to the devil wrath. One unperfectness shows me another, to make me frankly despise myself."

# THE LITTLE PRINCE

To be king and be powerful has some advantages, but in the back of your mind, there are always a few urgent questions. How long can I stay in power? Who will succeed me? Will my successor make me proud or cause me to lose face? And no matter if you are a CEO or a manager, you may well think as much about your succession as you do about your own death.

Succession in Shakespeare's time is simple. At least, if the king or queen gave birth to an heir to the throne. Royal blood is paramount. No child? Or did your child 'accidentally' not reach the age of eighteen? Then there would be an utterly entertaining battle for succession. If there is someone who can demonstrate how to make a mess of your own succession, it certainly is King Lear.

*"Meantime we shall express our darker purpose - give me the map there. Know that we have divided in three our kingdom, and 'tis our fast intent to shake all cares and business from our age, conferring them on younger strengths while we unburdened crawl toward death."* This is how Lear announces his abdication. With this

*measure, he steps away from the common practice in those days to stick to the throne until you dropped dead in front of it - a practice still celebrated by the British royal family four hundred years later. In itself, there is not much to argue about Lear's motivation: "We have this hour a constant will to publish our daughters' several dowers, that future strife may be prevented now." However, the execution leaves something to be desired and eventually leads to bitter battles ahead. Through his own stubbornness, Lear sees himself forced to give away his kingdom to what would appear to be his two most incompetent daughters. Within a short period of time, they break down the 'family business' and it collapses into chaos and perdition. The kingdom does not go down with the Lear family, but the king goes into his grave crazy as a bat. Again, the fate Shakespeare has in store for his main character is cruel. If only they had paid a little more attention and given some thought to what they did.*

It is not easy for Lear to put his money where his mouth is because he has always been powerful and actually does not really want it any other way. He finds it difficult to hand over control and, in fact, his message is: 'Come on ladies, let's get to work, but do not forget that daddy is still the boss.'

Handing over control of an organisation based on emotion as Lear wants to do is doomed to fail. Lear is unable to judge his daughters' abilities objectively and does not listen to his advisors. Listening to the sycophants trying to kiss their way up and ignoring objective feedback is just plain stupid. If the C-suite of an organisation is only surrounded by Yes-Men, you will only hear what you would like to hear.

In addition, Lear does not entirely think through what life will look like after retirement, making himself dependant on the charity of his daughters. Now that the spoil has been won, they no longer seem so sweet. England turns into a mess and others, like the king of France, see opportunities for their gain.

## GOD SAVE THE KING

Being a successor is a promotion but a succession also entails a significant leadership change in the organisation. Although King Lear's story is in particular similar to succession issues in family business, the problems and mistakes that he makes in the play are applicable to many organisations. There are plenty of people at the top who have worked for the organisation for a long time, having the same stature as Lear.

# SCENE 12

(An enormous boardroom, somewhere at the top floor of a skyscraper in a large city. The CEO is sitting in the largest chair, opposite him the management consultant. They are drinking iced tea.)

**Management consultant**: Your succession is reason for concern and not just because of your age. The imaging in the press is alarming.

**CEO**: I couldn't care less what these cockroaches are writing.

**Management** consultant: It does influence the share price. Recently in an interview your ex-girlfriend said that the only things you are still passionate about are football, sex, lobster and … (CEO interrupts.)

**CEO**: At least she is right about something.

**Management consultant**: But this all leads to the impression you don't care about the future of your company. What's your thought on that?

**CEO**: Nonsense. It is impossible not to care about my company because I am my company. These hands have built it but can break it into pieces as well. My ex's bullshit is just as ridiculous as the fairy tales of my children about my health. Do you see a demented old fool sitting in front of you? Do you? They're only after one thing and I am not going to give it to them. Not now. Not ever.

**Management consultant**: Your daughter…

(CEO interrupts him again.)

**CEO**: Yes? What about my daughter? And which one are we talking about anyway: the one who wants to stab me in the back or the one married to that excuse of a man?

**Management consultant**: The one you thought of as being your successor.

**CEO**: That's right: past tense. No more!

**Management consultant**: I understand your emotion but still, you've turned 87 recently and there are many rumours around your succession. The stock exchange expects clarity. When are you planning to do so?

**CEO**: Wall street? Screw them. I am not going to

die, so there is no point in having this discussion.
I think we are done here.
**Management consultant**: I really would like you
to…
(CEO interrupts him again.)
**CEO**: We're done, I said. Goodbye.

Family-run businesses in particular (in fact that is
exactly what a royal family is) face great risks when
it comes to succession. Before you know it, you are
losing customers, subject to a take-over because
leadership fails, or prone to internal chaos where the
competition sees an opportunity to win. But normal
organisations also run similar risks if they do not
have their succession strategy in place. Employees
do not necessarily expect to hear names of potential
successors or full transparency, but the absence of
a strategic, thoughtful and practical succession plan
is a big risk for both in the short and, certainly, in
the long term. An unclear process raises the levels
of gossip and potentially undermines the corporate
culture.

A change at the top makes everyone below think
about their priorities and worry about their job

security. Planning is key and it is all about preventing negative consequences for an organisation. Of course, bad succession plans draw attention earlier in the process. If Lear had a good plan, the play would have ended after five minutes. After all, just watching good news is boring. There is nothing as spectacular as a fight in the boardroom, a forced exit to make way for another colleague or the unexpected fall of a public darling.

## THE KING IS DEAD. LONG LIVE THE KING!

The first task of all who find themselves on top of the pyramid is to think about their succession and to ensure that a successor is prepared in case of an emergency. Conspiracy theorists strongly believe that such a process can help a new CEO to map out and eliminate his competitors. In order to prevent a Roman tragedy from happening, it is important that this process is supervised, for example by a supervisory board. This ensures that CEOs don't prepare successors whose only concern is the legacy of the mandate of their predecessor.

Lear does not get advice and makes mistakes he

could have prevented - the same mistakes that are still being made today. No one in court has any idea that Lear wants to resign. When he suddenly announces it, everyone is flabbergasted. All involved are completely taken by surprise but nevertheless have to come in action immediately, which is quite a challenge when you feel the proverbial knife on your throat. Lear has no well devised plan; he thinks it will be smooth sailing all the way and exactly in the direction he expects. His rigid attitude and blunt behaviour are a result of that. He has the strong belief that his idea is absolutely brilliant. He makes the mistake of ignoring his excellently qualified advisors. For example, Lear could have informed Kent in advance so that he could help him with the emotional side of running a family business. However, he chooses to take Kent completely by surprise, making it impossible for him to fix the King's the error. Fun drama on stage, but not very convenient in professional organisations where good planning and thoughtful processes are crucial.

## AFTER ME, THE DELUGE

How should it be done? To begin with, do not stick your head in the sand. No one is immortal, not even the greatest leaders. Every leader must think about when and under what circumstances he would ideally want to leave the organisation. The departure of a leader is a great moment to review the organisation again. Why do we do what we do? What do we do and how do we actually do it? The direction the organisation has to take is the best basis for a new leadership profile and will attract the best candidates. An excellent recruitment and selection process is therefore indispensable, just like some space in the same process for different opinions and insights. If someone wants to be a bit Leary and wants to stay in the organisation, then this new role must be clearly defined so that the successor has the pleasure but not the burden. Finally, make an objective choice. Enjoy the wealth of a choice of different candidates, but ultimately make that choice. Without proper succession planning strategy, you will break more than you love. The same applies to your colleagues too.

So, what if Shakespeare wants to help Lear with his

succession? He could allow Kent to have a meeting with all of the stakeholders to get a grip on the situation. He could make Lear think about the following questions: what kind of leadership does his kingdom need in the future? Is it a good idea to share this responsibility? A final possibility for Shakespeare is to hire the Stratford Consulting Group as external adviser to Lear to review his plan.

## HEY! THAT'S NO WAY TO SAY GOODBYE

When it comes to succession in the British monarchy, most scions enjoy the advantage of a dead predecessor. It is not possible to reign from your grave. In modern organisations, that is often quite different. The person who leaves their job as CEO gains a different position in the organisation or has influence in another way. Take the example of the Dutch family-run business Vroom & Dreesmann, which, until recently, populated Dutch towns with its massive department stores for over a century. In the last two decades of the previous century, the company turned into a stage where a Shakespearean-like succession drama unfolded.

Anton Dreesmann takes control of the company after the death of his older brother in a fatal accident. It is a position Anton has always dreamt of. He has a reputation of a powerful and sometimes merciless entrepreneur. His leadership allows the company to flourish until the inevitable moment arrives that he has to hand over control. Anton is not fond of thinking about his succession. At the age of forty-eight, just recovering from his first heart attack, he says: "Having a crown prince is deadly for a company. A good crown prince becomes restless. He will wait for your heart attack."

Not every family business has a crown prince lined up and in the case of Vroom & Dreesmann the leadership of the company is ultimately passed on to an outsider. The outsider quickly gets to the root cause of all evil in regard to the future of department stores and the position of the company. A plan is being developed and a reorganisation deployed. However, a good transfer and transition of decision-making is not possible, because from his sick bed - he has had a cerebral haemorrhage – Anton becomes a Saboteur. He interferes in a way that would not have been misplaced in a Shakespeare play: "I have seen my testament be opened. But I pulled myself up on my own gravestone to show myself. They did not count on that."

Anton Dreesmann and King Lear are rather similar in their approach: "A silly old man who still wants to act with the authority he has given away." So for those who think they can stay in power forever a last final short lesson from the same play: "This policy and reverence of age makes the world bitter to the best of our times, keeps our fortunes from us till our oldness cannot relish them. I begin to find an idle and fond bondage in the oppression of aged tyranny, who sways not as it hath power but as it is suffered. Come to me, that of this I may speak more. If our father would sleep till I waked him, you should enjoy half his revenue forever."

## CONGRATULATIONS (I THINK)

Henry V's father, whom we met in Act One, is not really confident in having his son as his successor and secretly even thinks about surpassing him for another. In a father to son meeting he tells him: "Thou seekest the greatness that will overwhelm thee." He speaks of experience because he knows what you will experience once you are on the throne. He himself came to power by a coup and had no idea how to deal with the situation he got himself into. After forcing his opponent to step down, he has him assassinated in prison not much later. Cleaning up the mess makes him look tidy and it is also better for his peace of mind. Predecessors who stick around in the organisation are often a stumbling block.

The promotion paradox is that you need the right people as managers to promote the right people. Making a mistake with the first will have irrevocably negative consequences for the second. Managers and leaders have a crucial role to play in promotions and succession. People are working for people not for organisations. If you want to retain the crown princes and -princesses in your organisation, excellent management is a critical matter. Do not promote just anyone to a managerial position and have a close look in the mirror if you want to raise your finger to become a manager. The idea that anyone can lead is too often an accepted belief. You have been educated or trained for most of the work you do. Managing is a profession as well and requires training. We expect a lawyer to have a law degree. A marketer must have had a strong marketing training. In addition to training one must have affinity with and passion for their profession to be successful. It is rather odd that this seems less likely to apply to the average manager. Anyone can be a manager, right? No? Then continue to train and develop your managers.

King Lear and Othello are absolute masterpieces in the (playwright) literature, but should also have a top spot in the management literature. The characters give insightful lessons about promotion and succession and especially about how it should not be done. If you see a colleague with a sinister Iago look in their eyes after missing a promotion, be worried. Be worried if you see colleagues fighting over a seat in the boardroom. You now know what can go wrong, the dramas that could happen as a result of rash decision making and / or inadequate processes. In general, the more trust there is in an organisation the fewer rules and procedures are needed. However, if it is about promotion, demotion and succession, it is very important to have the processes well-organised. This will elevate that trust. A classic catch 22 – or, in proper English, the problem of the chicken and the egg.

Should you be happy or not if you are being promoted, take a parity step or if you are considered to be a successor? Of course, you should be. If you are in fact really happy with that. You must earn a promotion, allow yourself to take a parity step and you are not easily considered in a succession plan.

And you? Are you ready to climb up that ladder? Do you know who your competitors are and how to befriend them? Do you really need friends if you finally have your own office? Are you sitting in the right chair? Is that chair perhaps a little bit too comfortable? But above all: are you still happy with what you do?

# EPILOGUE

*"There is no art to find the mind's construction in the face. He was a gentleman on whom I built, an absolute trust."*

**Macbeth**

The common thread in this book is trust - trust in the people you work with, your colleagues, your manager, the director. That can be very difficult, because they are different from you. Every Act in this book is about trust. Trust in your team. Trust that everyone has equal opportunities in your organisation and that diversity is important. Being confident that there is respect for your norms and values. To know that it is safe to speak up because you work in an open organisation. The confidence that your organisation makes the right choices when it comes to your and your colleagues' career.

In a world where change is going faster and faster and organisations feel challenged to change as quickly as their environment, you cannot do without trust. Trust to try out and break new organisational structures. Trusting the agility of your colleagues. Trust in cooperation to enable innovation. Every organisation evolves around its employees and the goals they need to achieve together. That can only be done with trust.

Shakespeare plays with trust. He shows how organisations and people grow and flourish. He also shows the tragedy in organisations lacking trust. You do not have to be insane to trust others. Not at all. So do not hesitate to rely on yourself and others. For, as Shakespeare writes, "Our doubts are traitors, and makes us lose the good we oft might win by fearing to attempt."

# THANK YOU

*"Take each man's censure, but reserve thy judgment."*

**Hamlet**

Martine Hamstra, Patricia Daniels, Cíntia Taylor, Alice van Gorp, Roeland Windig, Thomas Gallay, Dirk-Jan Koeman, Jan-Maarten Rovers, Michiel van de Watering, Vivian Tevreden, Michelle van Gunst, Angelique Lombarts, Gary Blufpand, Arie de Rooij, Vincent Verkoelen, Carolien van der Ven, Bram Gerrits, Geerhard Bolte, Ana Rhodes, Richard Olivier and of course William Shakespeare.

# SOURCES

This book is based on research, my own experiences and a significant number of (on-line) publications about leadership, diversity, behaviour, HR management and communication. Below you will find an overview of the most important literature that was used.

- Armstrong, Jane. *The Arden dictionary of Shakespeare quotations*. Bloomsbury. 2010.
- Bate, Jonathan & Rasmussen Eric. *William Shakespeare complete works*. The Royal Shakespeare Company. 2007.
- Bryson, Bill. *Shakespeare*. Harper Collins. 2007.
- Corrigan, Paul. *Shakespeare on management*. Kogan Page. 1999.
- Crystal, Ben. *Shakespeare on toast*. Icon books. 2008.
- Dickson, Andrew. *The Globe guide to Shakespeare*. Profile books. 2016.
- Etzold, Veit. *'Powerplays: What Shakespeare can

*teach on leadership'*. Business Strategy Series, vol. 13, no. 2. 2012.

- Foley, Elizabeth & Coates, Beth. *Shakespeare for grown-ups*. Square peg. 2014.
- Gomez-Mejia, Luis. *Managing Human Resources*. Prentice Hall. 2001.
- Horst, Anthon van der a.o. *Groot psychologisch modellenboek*. Van Duuren Management. 2010.
- Kets de Vries, Manfred. *Leiderschap ontraadseld*. Sdu uitgevers, 2006.
- Klinkenberg, Rob. *Kings of War*. Athenaeum. 2015.
- Lammers, Cor a.o. *Organisaties vergelijkenderwijs*. Het Spectrum. 1997.
- Laloux, Frederic. *Reinventing organisations*. LannooCampus. 2016.
- Lencioni, Patrick. *The five dysfunctions of a team*. Jossey-Bass. 2002.
- Novey, Marianne. *Shakespeare's outsiders*. Oxford University Press. 2013.
- Olivier, Richard. *Inspirational leadership*. Nicholas Brealy Publishing. 2013.
- Robbins, Stephen. *Organizational behavior*. Prentice Hall. 1989.

- Rosen, Michael. *What's so special about Shakespeare?* Walker books. 2001.
- Shakespeare, William. *Hamlet*.
- Shakespeare, William. *Henry V*.
- Shakespeare, William. *Julius Caesar*.
- Shakespeare, William. *King Lear*.
- Shakespeare, William. *Macbeth*.
- Shakespeare, William. *Othello*.
- Welch, Jack. *Winning*. Harper Business. 2005
- Wells, Stanley a.o. *The Shakespeare book*. Dorling Kindersey. 2015.
- Whitney, John & Packer, Tina. *Shakespeare's lessons in leadership and management*. Simon and Schuster. 2000.

Published by Haystack Publishing

P.O. Box 308
5301 BT Zaltbommel
The Netherlands

www.haystack.nl/shakespeare
needle@haystack.nl

English version copyright © 2018 by Wiemer Renkema

Author: Wiemer Renkema
Original title: Managen of niet, dat is de vraag
Translation: Patricia Daniels and Cíntia Taylor
Illustrations: Debbie Brok
Book cover design: Levin den Boer
Interior design: Debbie Brok

ISBN: 9789461262752 | NUR: 801

www.ingramcontent.com/pod-product-compliance
Lightning Source LLC
Chambersburg PA
CBHW051210090426
42740CB00022B/3450